MINORITIES

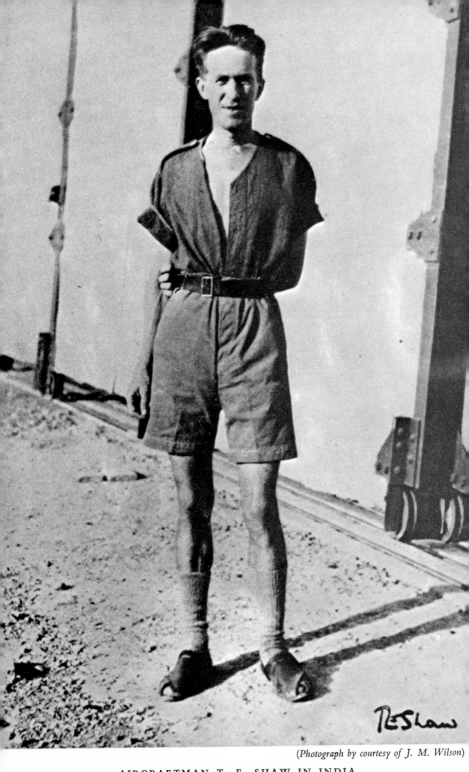

(Photograph by courtesy of J. M. Wilson)

AIRCRAFTMAN T. E. SHAW IN INDIA

T. E. Lawrence

MINORITIES

Good Poems by Small Poets
and Small Poems by Good Poets

EDITED BY J. M. WILSON

PREFACE BY C. DAY LEWIS

Doubleday & Company, Inc.
Garden City, New York

1972

By T. E. Lawrence

CRUSADER CASTLES

THE WILDERNESS OF ZIN
(with C. Leonard Woolley)

SEVEN PILLARS OF WISDOM

THE MINT

For permission to reproduce copyright material, I gratefully acknowledge the following: A. D. Peters & Co., for extracts from 'Stanzas written on Battersea Bridge during a South-Westerly Gale' by Hilaire Belloc, reprinted from *Verses* (Duckworth, London, 1910); the Literary Trustees of Walter de la Mare, and the Society of Authors as their representative, for 'Arabia' and 'The Song of Shadows' by Walter de la Mare, reprinted from *The Complete Poems of Walter de la Mare* (Faber, London, 1969); Mr. Robert Graves, for his poem 'A Forced Music', reprinted from *Whipperginny* (Heinemann, London, 1923); The Macmillan Company, for 'To the Moon', 'When I set out for Lyonesse', 'The Ivy-Wife' and 'The Impercipient' by Thomas Hardy, reprinted from *The Collected Poems of Thomas Hardy* (Copyright 1925 by The Macmillan Company), and for the final chorus from *The Dynasts* (Copyright 1904 by The Macmillan Company, renewed 1931 by Florence E. Hardy); The Macmillan Company, for 'Eve', 'The Mystery' and 'The Moor' by Ralph Hodgson, reprinted from *Poems By Ralph Hodgson* (Copyright 1917 by The Macmillan Company, renewed 1945 by Ralph Hodgson); Holt, Rinehart and Winston, Inc., for 'Epitaph on an Army of Mercenaries', 'Eight O'Clock' and 'Revolution' by A. E. Housman, reprinted from *The Collected Poems of A. E. Housman* (Copyright 1922 by Holt, Rinehart and Winston, Inc. Copyright 1950 by Barclays Bank Ltd.); Jonathan Cape Ltd., for 'Failure' by Laurence Housman, reprinted from *Green Arras* (John Lane, London, 1896); Mrs. George Bambridge and Doubleday & Company, Inc., for 'My New-Cut Ashlar' by Rudyard Kipling, reprinted from the book *Life's Handicap* by Rudyard Kipling; The Viking Press, Inc., for 'Ballad of a Wilful Woman' and excerpts from the Foreword and the Argument of *Look! We have come through!* by D. H. Lawrence, *The Complete Poems of D. H. Lawrence*, copyright © 1964, 1971 by Angelo Ravagli and C. M. Weekley, Executors of the Estate of Frieda Lawrence Ravagli; Mr. A. W. Lawrence, for extracts from the 'Oxford' draft of *Seven Pillars of Wisdom* (1922); the Editor of the *New Statesman*, for 'Skias Onar' by F. L. Lucas, reprinted from the *New Statesman* (9.viii.1924); the Executors of the late Alice Meynell, for 'Parentage', 'Via, et Veritas, et Vita' and ' "I am the way" ' by Alice Meynell, reprinted from *The Poems of Alice Meynell: Complete Edition* (Burns & Oates, London, 1923); Mr. John Crowe Ransom and Holt, Rinehart and Winston, Inc., for 'The Lover', reprinted from *Poems about God* by John Crowe Ransom (Copyright 1919 by Holt, Rinehart and Winston, Inc. Copyright 1947 by John Crowe Ransom); The Viking Press, Inc., for 'Everyone Sang', 'Limitations', 'Memory' and 'The Dug-Out' by Siegfried Sassoon, reprinted from *Collected Poems* by Siegfried Sassoon. Copyright 1920 by E. P. Dutton & Co.; renewed 1948 by Siegfried Sassoon. Reprinted by permission of The Viking Press, Inc.; The Macmillan Company, for 'The Snare' by James Stephens, reprinted from *Collected Poems* by James Stephens (Copyright 1915 by The Macmillan Company, renewed 1943 by James Stephens); George G. Harrap & Co. Ltd. for 'The Great Misgiving' by Sir William Watson, reprinted from *The Poems of Sir William Watson 1878-1935* (Harrap, London, 1936); Miss Ann Wolfe, for 'The Harlot I', reprinted from *Requiem* (Ernest Benn, London, 1927); and The Macmillan Company, for 'A Faery Song' and 'The Lake Isle of Innisfree' by W. B. Yeats, reprinted from *The Collected Poems of W. B. Yeats* (Copyright 1906 by The Macmillan Company, renewed 1934 by William Butler Yeats).

ISBN: 0-385-07001-2
LIBRARY OF CONGRESS CATALOG CARD NUMBER 77-186036
COPYRIGHT © 1971 BY TIMES NEWSPAPERS LTD
ALL RIGHTS RESERVED
PRINTED IN THE UNITED STATES OF AMERICA
FIRST EDITION IN THE UNITED STATES OF AMERICA

Contents

Acknowledgments

I should like to thank Mr Escombe for his unsparing co-operation, and especially for having identified all but a few of the poems. Mr Harold Evans, Editor of the *Sunday Times*, and Mrs Catherine Storr of Jonathan Cape have responded with considerable tact, patience and generosity to my various requirements. I should also like to thank Mr A. W. Lawrence for permission to use copyright material, as well as for his kindness and encouragement.

The following libraries have allowed me to quote from unpublished letters: the Codrington Library, by permission of the Warden and Fellows of All Souls College, Oxford; the Bodleian Library; the Library of the British Museum; Harvard University Library; and the Alexander Turnbull Library, Wellington, New Zealand. In addition, I am grateful to the Executors of the recipients of letters for permission to quote from copies embargoed in the Bodleian Library. For leave to quote from *T. E. Lawrence to his Biographer Robert Graves* (Faber, London, 1938) and from a review by Lawrence published in the *Spectator* of August 6th, 1937, I should like to thank Mr Robert Graves and the Editor of the *Spectator*, respectively.

For permission to reproduce copyright material, I gratefully acknowledge the following: A. D. Peters & Co., for extracts from 'Stanzas written on Battersea Bridge during a South-Westerly Gale' by Hilaire Belloc, reprinted from *Verses* (Duckworth, London, 1910); the Literary Trustees of Walter de la Mare, and The Society of Authors as their representative, for 'Arabia' and 'The Song of Shadows' by Walter de la Mare, reprinted from *The Complete Poems of Walter de la Mare* (Faber, London, 1969); Mr Robert Graves, for his poem 'A Forced Music', reprinted from *Whipperginny* (Heinemann, London, 1923); the Trustees of the Hardy Estate, Macmillan & Co. Ltd, London, and The Macmillan Company of Canada Ltd, for 'To the Moon', 'When I set out for Lyonesse', 'The Ivy-Wife' and 'The Impercipient' by Thomas Hardy, reprinted from *The Collected Poems of Thomas Hardy* (Macmillan, London, 1960), and for the final chorus from *The Dynasts* (Macmillan, London, 1908); Mrs Ralph Hodgson, Macmillan & Co. Ltd, London, and The Macmillan Company of Canada Ltd, for 'Eve', 'The Mystery' and 'The Moor' by Ralph Hodgson, reprinted from *Collected Poems* (Macmillan, London, 1961); The Society of Authors as Literary Representative of the Estate of A. E. Housman, and Jonathan Cape Ltd as publishers of the *Collected Poems*, for 'Epitaph on an Army of Mercenaries', 'Eight O'Clock' and 'Revolution' by A. E. Housman, reprinted from *The Collected Poems of A. E. Housman* (Cape, London, 1942); Jonathan Cape Ltd, for 'Failure' by Laurence Housman, reprinted from *Green Arras* (John Lane, London, 1896); Mrs George Bambridge and Macmillan & Co. Ltd, London, for 'My New-Cut Ashlar' by Rudyard Kipling, reprinted from *Life's Handicap* (Macmillan, London, 1891); Laurence Pollinger Ltd, the Estate of the late Mrs Frieda Lawrence and William Heinemann Ltd, for 'Ballad of a Wilful Woman' and excerpts from the Foreword and the Argument of *Look! We have come through!* by D. H. Lawrence, reprinted from *The Complete Poems of D. H. Lawrence* (Heinemann, London, 1964); Mr A. W. Lawrence, for extracts from the 'Oxford' draft of *Seven Pillars of Wisdom* (1922) and from *The Mint* (Cape, London, 1955) by T. E. Lawrence; the Seven Pillars Trust, for extracts from *Seven Pillars of Wisdom* (Cape, London, 1935) by T. E. Lawrence; the T. E. Lawrence Letters Trust, for extracts from published and unpublished letters; the Editor of the *New Statesman*, for 'Skias Onar' by F. L. Lucas, reprinted from the *New Statesman* (9.viii.1924); the Executors of

8

the late Alice Meynell, for 'Parentage', 'Via, et Veritas, et Vita' and ' "I am the Way" ' by Alice Meynell, reprinted from *The Poems of Alice Meynell: Complete Edition* (Burns & Oates, London, 1923); Mr John Crowe Ransom, for his poem 'The Lover', reprinted from *Poems about God* (Holt, New York, 1919); Mr G. T. Sassoon, for 'Everyone Sang', 'Limitations', 'Memory' and 'The Dug-Out' by Siegfried Sassoon, reprinted from *The Collected Poems of Siegfried Sassoon* (Faber, London, 1961); Mrs Iris Wise, Macmillan & Co. Ltd, London, and The Macmillan Company of Canada Ltd, for 'The Snare' by James Stephens, reprinted from *Collected Poems* (Macmillan, London, 1954); George G. Harrap & Co. Ltd, for 'The Great Misgiving' by Sir William Watson, reprinted from *The Poems of Sir William Watson 1878–1935* (Harrap, London, 1936); Miss Ann Wolfe, for 'The Harlot: I', reprinted from *Requiem* (Ernest Benn, London, 1927); and Mr M. B. Yeats and Macmillan & Co. Ltd, London, for 'A Faery Song' and 'The Lake Isle of Innisfree' by W. B. Yeats, reprinted from *The Collected Poems of W. B. Yeats* (Macmillan, London, 1950).

I was invited to take over the editorial work on *Minorities* from Mr Colin Simpson in May 1970, and I must apologize to anyone who contributed to the project in its early stages whom I have not thanked by name. My approach differed entirely from Mr Simpson's and his editorial work is not reflected here. Nevertheless, it is doubtful that *Minorities* would now appear in print but for his initiative in 1968.

Finally I should like to thank all those, not already named, who have helped me in research on T. E. Lawrence, especially the staffs of the libraries I have used.

J.M.W.

Abbreviations used in the References

A.T.   Alexander Turnbull Library, Wellington, New Zealand

B.   Bodleian Library, Oxford

B:L.H.   'T. E. Lawrence to his Biographer Liddell Hart'. Part II of *T. E. Lawrence to his Biographers Robert Graves and Liddell Hart* (Cassell, London, 1963)

B.M.   British Museum

B.(R)   From the T. E. Lawrence papers placed in the Bodleian Library by the T. E. Lawrence Trustees under an embargo until the year 2000

B:R.G.   'T. E. Lawrence to his Biographer Robert Graves'. Part I of *T. E. Lawrence to his Biographers Robert Graves and Liddell Hart* (Cassell, London, 1963)

C. F. Shaw   Letters to Mrs Bernard Shaw in the British Museum, Additional MS. 45903, 45904

D.G.   *The Letters of T. E. Lawrence*, ed. David Garnett. New edn with some corrections and a Foreword by B. H. Liddell Hart (Spring Books, London, 1964)

F.   *T. E. Lawrence by his Friends*, ed. A. W. Lawrence (Cape, London, 1937)

H.   Houghton Library, Harvard University

H.B.   *Architecture and Personalities* by Sir Herbert Baker (Country Life, London, 1944)

H.L.   *The Home Letters of T. E. Lawrence and his Brothers*, ed. M. R. Lawrence (Blackwell, Oxford, 1954)

H.W.	*Genius of Friendship: 'T. E. Lawrence'* by Henry Williamson (Faber, London, 1941)
Mint	*The Mint: A day-book of the R.A.F. Depot between August and December 1922 with later Notes* by 352087 A/C Ross [T. E. Lawrence] (Cape, London, 1955)
O.A.	*Oriental Assembly*, ed. A. W. Lawrence. Miscellaneous writings of T. E. Lawrence (Williams and Norgate, London, 1939)
S.L.	*The Secret Lives of Lawrence of Arabia* by Phillip Knightley and Colin Simpson (Nelson, London, 1969)
S.P.	*Seven Pillars of Wisdom: a triumph* by T. E. Lawrence (Cape, London, 1935)
S.P.(O)	*Seven Pillars of Wisdom: a triumph* by T. E. Lawrence. The 'Oxford' draft, printed in 1922
S.T.	*Sunday Times*, London
V.R.	*Portrait of T. E. Lawrence: The Lawrence of the Seven Pillars of Wisdom* by Vyvyan Richards (Cape, London, 1936)

Preface

The admirable essay by Mr J. M. Wilson which follows has set right a number of points about T. E. Lawrence's character and actions. One of these has to do with his anthology, *Minorities*. Mr Wilson has established that Lawrence did not start copying out these poems till 1919: they were copied into a small, red leather-bound book, 112 of them, some complete, others in extracts, neither titles nor authors' names given, over a period of about eight years. Lawrence had carried *The Oxford Book of English Verse* with him during the final stages of the Arab revolt, and it was from this book that about 30 of the poems were taken which appear in the early pages of *Minorities*.

Writing to Mrs Bernard Shaw in 1927, he said he had chosen 'the minor poems I wanted. Some are the small poems of big men: others the better poems of small men. One necessary qualification was that they should be in a minor key; another that they should sing a little bit.'

This presents us with one of those enigmas which T.E. scattered so freely about him, to tease and mystify posterity. He cannot surely have considered Wordsworth, Coleridge, Shelley and Keats as 'small men'; but equally it is impossible to imagine him rating the 'Intimations' ode, 'Kubla Khan', 'Prometheus Unbound' or the 'Ode to a Nightingale' as '*small* poems of big men'. It has been represented to me that his criteria for judgment changed as time went on: yet as late as 1927 he wrote to Edward Garnett about *Minorities* as 'good poems by small poets, or small poems by good poets'.

T.E. was always a great reader of poetry, as the more than 300 volumes of verse at Clouds Hill attested; and he read critically, if idiosyncratically. Can we gauge his state of mind at any given period by the kind of poems he chose then for his book? This raises another question: is one most drawn to poems which reflect one's state of mind, or to poems which counter it? The earlier poems in *Minorities*, which do answer to his definition — 'in a minor key' — could indeed be said to tune with the disillusionment and exhaustion he felt immediately after the war. It is easy to understand why at that time he should prefer minor poetry to the great poems which stretch and batter the imagination. On the other hand the 'sweet tooth' in poetry, which he admitted more than once to possessing, runs *counter* to the puritanism of his character and the asceticism of his life. So where are we? I myself do not find it very rewarding to read autobiography between the lines of this anthology. ·

Its taste, we may safely say, is founded on what T. E. most liked at his most impressionable age, and this gives *Minorities* a faintly Ninetyish-plus-Edwardian flavour. At the same time, reading through this collection, I was struck by the way he so often did not choose the hackneyed, much-anthologized pieces but ones which are fresh, or renew their freshness from the context in which he placed them. He was certainly not confined to the taste of his youth: he read widely and stayed open even to the work of my own generation. He liked poetry which had a lyric movement, and this partly accounted for his depreciation of the Metaphysical poets. The turning against stylized or 'intellectual' verse, his increasing sense of the value of simple language, seems to have dated from the period when T.E. joined the Tank Corps and found more opportunity for relaxation: it also goes hand in hand with an interest in reading for the 'common man' he showed when he was a mechanic in the Air Force. The change-over from the highly wrought style of *Seven Pillars* to the plain language of *The Mint* illustrates the same point.

The 'literary' quality of *Seven Pillars* has alienated some critics of recent years. T.E.'s move towards a simpler way of writing may be related with his inclination to value a poem for its content rather more than its technical merits (he was living at a time when the view that form and content are inseparable was not obligatory). But the reader must decide how far this emphasis on *what* a poem says, and the playing-down of how it says it, are noticeable throughout *Minorities*. T.E.'s expressed veneration for Blake and for Thomas Hardy, whose simplicities of style and depths of meaning are evident, and his liking for Edward Thomas and Siegfried Sassoon, by no means keep him from including a good many poems of a more flowery and shallow nature.

His own change of style was another facet of T.E.'s perfectionism; and this in its turn contrasts with the fascination which the imperfect held for him. Works 'in the Titan class', he wrote, are composed 'with a strain that dislocates the writer, and exhausts the reader'. In minor works, on the other hand, 'their cracks and imperfections serve an artistic end in themselves'. On his love for William Morris, T.E. said, 'the charm and comfort of imperfection makes up for most of the failures of the world. We admire the very great, but love the less.' His continuing love for this poet links up with the great interest in medievalism which coloured his mind before the war, and with the chivalrous, aspiring spirit which accompanied many of his generation into it.

Although there were few references to poetry in his *Letters* (Cape, London, 1938), a good deal of unpublished material has since come to light which extends my knowledge of his thoughts on poetry. These are sometimes contradictory, sometimes perverse (how often the word 'impish' crops up in anecdotes about T.E.), always independent-minded. His generalizations could be wide of the mark; but, in criticizing a friend's poems, he was very much on the spot, with great attention to details of technique. As a tipster he was by no means infallible: in 1934 he wrote to me, 'Auden makes me fear that he will not write much more. Spender might, on

the other hand, write too much.' He was remarkably perci-
pient about writers as different as D. H. Lawrence and James
Stephens. He came to admire Yeats greatly; but of his earlier
work had said, Yeats 'lacks vulgarity ... and consequently
lacks the sense to avoid vulgarity'. He foxed Robert Graves
and Laura Riding by assuming the mask of a low-brow. He
could find 'In Memoriam' lacking in music. His dislikes can
seem as unwarrantable and violent as some of his enthusiasms.

Minorities was not intended for publication: but, if it had
been, I see no reason to suppose that Lawrence's choice of
poems would have been substantially different. Being out of
sympathy with those persons who have sought, by diminishing
him as a scholar, a writer or a military leader, to cut him down
to their own size, I maintain my conviction that he was an
exceptional human being, and that anything which came from
his hand deserves our interest and respect.

C. DAY LEWIS

Introduction

Despite his lifelong interest in poetry, T. E. Lawrence left behind very little comment[1] compared to his extensive criticism of contemporary prose, and this anthology is itself the clearest index we are likely to discover of his taste in poetry. Yet *Minorities* provides only partial evidence, for Lawrence chose these poems more for their matter than their manner (it was in these terms that he distinguished content from style). Consequently, readers who are interested in his literary judgment may be disappointed by the collection, but anyone familiar with *Seven Pillars of Wisdom, The Mint* and his letters, will recognize in these poems many ideas also expressed by Lawrence. The purpose of this introduction is to set *Minorities* against the background of Lawrence's developing outlook.

Minorities was, Lawrence wrote, 'my private anthology, which necessity and much travelling compelled me to select and copy into a small note-book for myself'. After the war his interest in poetry had widened, especially towards contemporary writing, and 'I found that not even the *Oxford Book of English Verse*[2] [which he had carried during much of the Arab Revolt] quite fitted my whim. So I took to copying, carelessly, in a little Morrell-bound note-book … the minor poems I wanted.'

Slightly less than a third of his choice came from the Oxford anthology. These provide, in the order he originally copied them, twenty-four of the first

27.iv.27
to E. Garnett, B.(R)

17.xi.27
to C. F. Shaw, B.M.

---

[1] Material from his writings bearing on *Minorities* is included in the Notes. For many of the poems, however, it has not been possible to find relevant statements.

[2] His copy was a 1915 reprint of the edition of 1900.

thirty-seven, but at most nine of the remaining seventy-five poems.

17.xi.27
to C. F.
Shaw, S.L.,
p. 260

He wrote: 'Some are the small poems of big men: others the better poems of small men', and there is no suggestion that the collection was intended to represent everything he admired in poetry. No author who habitually improved his style through repeated critical revision, as Lawrence did, could fail to see the literary shortcomings of some of these poems, indeed he criticized several in his letters. They were undoubtedly chosen because they reflected his personal feelings and ideas at the time—ideas he often wrote about, and would have expressed in poetry had he been able.

He told Charlotte Shaw, to whom he gave *Minorities* in 1927 (in return for her own private anthology of medita-

Ibid.

tions), that 'Its poems have each of them had a day with me. That little hackneyed Clough,[1] for instance, about light coming up in the west also: I read that at Umtaiye, when the Deraa expedition was panicking and in misery: and it closely fitted my trust in Allenby, out of sight beyond the hills. There's all that sort of thing, for me, behind the simple words.' In most instances such a particular association cannot be established, but this does not remove the biographical interest of the poems. The collection reflects his outlook powerfully, partly because of the strength and clarity of his feelings, but also through an intended coherence. In the

Ibid.

same letter to Charlotte Shaw he wrote: 'One necessary qualification was that they should be in a minor key ...'

24.ix.22
to R. Graves,
B:R.G.,
p. 21

In another letter, to Robert Graves, he is more explicit: 'I wish everyone had calmness after their storms ... So some day do write a sunset poem for my benefit. Did I ever show you my private anthology? *Minorities*, I called it. You are not in it yet, because you haven't done that special note which runs through it.'

The poems he chose were often the expression of deep

---

[1] 'Say not the struggle naught availeth', No. 52.

18

feelings, of nostalgia, exhaustion, self-condemnation, of faith and forebodings of death. He was conscious of these unguarded emotions and both reticent and apologetic about his choice. He never showed *Minorities* to Graves, though he warned him: 'you'll be astonished at my sweet tooth, if ever you see that discreditable collection'. He thought Edward Garnett more likely to sympathize, and announced soon after their first meeting: 'Next time I come ... I'll bring my box of moral éclairs with me, and we shall lick them together. You'll find enough sugar in that anthology to make six people sick: but my stomach is that of seven men. Boasting again!' Even more revealing was his apology to Charlotte Shaw: 'The worst is you do not like minor poetry: so that perhaps the weakness of spirit in this collection will only anger you: and then my notebook will not be a fair return for your notebook. In my eyes it is: for I'm not so intellectual as to put brain-work above feeling: indeed as you know, I don't like these subdivisions of that essential unity, man.'

17.xi.27 to C. F. Shaw, B.M.

In October 1922, when the notebook was about half full, a letter to Garnett describes the common purpose with which he had tried to express in *Minorities* the personal and philosophical ideas running through *Seven Pillars*:

'My mind on literature is not yet crisp. I have looked in poetry (the crown and head, the only essential branch of letters) everywhere for satisfaction: and haven't found it. Instead I have made that private collection of bonbons: chocolate éclairs of the spirit: whereas I wanted a meal. Failing poetry I chased my fancied meal through prose, and found everywhere good little stuff, and only a few men who had honestly tried to be greater than mankind: and only their strainings and wrestlings really fill my stomach.

'I can't write poetry: so in prose I aimed at providing a meal for the fellow-seekers with myself. For this the whole experience, and emanations and surroundings (background and foreground) of a man are necessary. Whence the many facets of my book, its wild mop of side-scenes and side issues: the prodigality and profuseness: and the indigestibility of the dish. They were, when done, deliberate: and the book is a summary of what I have thought and done and made of myself in these first thirty years. Primarily it's that, and not a work of art ...'

It would be a great mistake, and indeed naive, to assume that Lawrence accepted or identified himself with these poems in their entirety. Sometimes only a fragment of their content or his highly subjective interpretation determined his choice. He said of poetry that 'the reader can put into it as much of his own subtlety and desire as he pleases'; and again, 'out of most concerts I get one or two or three exquisite moments when myself goes suddenly empty, the entire consciousness taking flight into space upon these vibrations of perfect sound. Each time lasts an instant only: more, and I should die, for it holds still my breath and blood and vital fluid. Just so the ecstacy of a poem lies in the few words here and there—an affair of seconds.'

24.xii.27
to R. Graves,
B:R.G.,
p. 142
Mint, II,
Ch. 2, p. 105

Lawrence often used such 'moments' from poetry to enrich his own writing through literary allusion: 'choosing out of each beloved phrase just the key-word or two, so that the rest echoes at once in the recognising mind.' In 1927 he explained how *Seven Pillars* came to contain 'its comprehensive anthology of echoes':

(1934)
to Sir H.
Baker,
H.B., p. 26

21.iv.27
to C. F.
Shaw, B.M.

'By the way it was my literary method, in making the ms now in the Bodleian, to take its destroyed original, paragraph by paragraph, and to dwell on each till it contained some one sentence, or cadence, or word only, which gave me pleasure. One per paragraph was the ration: because if each sentence had been pleasurable the thing would have become a surfeit. Also a true history of a real proceeding could hardly be written so selectively as that. Now in 90%

of cases this point which gave me pleasure was a quotation more or less disguised.'

In his autobiographical writings there are occasional allusions taken from poems in *Minorities*. These illuminate on the one hand the essential metaphor or quality of the poem, and on the other the circumstance in his life, sometimes an enduring circumstance, which gave it meaning.[1]

There is one special respect in which *Minorities* makes an essential contribution to any biographical study of Lawrence. This does not depend on its contents, except in the broadest sense, but on the timing of its compilation in relation to other biographical evidence. This question of timing must therefore be discussed in some detail.

Lawrence was a prolific letter-writer throughout his adult life except for the period between the autumn of 1916 and the summer of 1922. In the six missing years he fought the Arabian campaigns and wrote successive drafts of *Seven Pillars*. The events of the first two years of this interval are covered by *Seven Pillars*, and from this time until 1922 there is considerable official documentation of his military and political activities (released in 1968[2]). There is, however, almost no material of a personal nature before the period of *The Mint*, which records his experiences and feelings following enlistment in 1922. There is therefore a very important gap in biographical information, usually assumed to begin after the fall of Damascus in October 1918, described in the closing pages of *Seven Pillars*. His biographers have not found in the book convincing reasons for his later behaviour, and instead have attributed this to unknown events or to some mental disturbance during the undocumented period of 1919–22.

[1] Two interesting examples are given in notes 12 and 68 (see pp. 250 and 256).

[2] Almost all biographies of Lawrence were written before this, and it is still too soon to know what conclusions will be reached from detailed examination of the new material.

The first poems in *Minorities* show, however, that at the very beginning of this period, in 1919, Lawrence already had feelings of depression and self-condemnation very similar to those expressed in *The Mint* and in letters written after 1922. The anthology therefore provides unequivocal evidence that the elusive cause of his personal crisis arose during the Desert War.

This evidence must lead to a reappraisal of *Seven Pillars* as a biographical source. In the introductory chapter Lawrence said that 'the history is not of the Arab movement, but of me in it'. On this basis it might seem reasonable to assume that the autobiographical account in *Seven Pillars* was essentially a complete one. But there is ample evidence that many of Lawrence's personal feelings and reactions were omitted. He hoped to create a literary masterpiece, knowing that 'the story I have to tell is one of the most splendid ever given a man for writing'. In order to impose a dramatic integrity on the diffuse central narrative, he suppressed many autobiographical elements which had no direct connection with the campaign. For example, he barely mentioned his presence at the Allied entry into Jerusalem, which was not in the Arab sphere of operations, commenting only that the ceremony at the Jaffa Gate 'for me was the supreme moment of the war'.

There is certainly a growing sense of personal misgiving in *Seven Pillars*. Vyvyan Richards discerned in it the makings of a great tragedy. Lawrence replied: 'I tried to bring this out, just this side of egotism, as a second note running through the book after Chapter V,[1] and increasing slowly towards the close, but it would be a fault in scale to represent the Arab Revolt mainly as a personal tragedy to me.' The assumption that the first post-war years contain a break in Lawrence's life during which he changed radically is a fallacy. Together with this evidence, the tenor of the early

O.A., p. 142

1922
to V.
Richards,
V.R., p. 186

S.P.,
Ch. LXXXI,
p. 453

1922
to V.
Richards,
V.R., p. 188

[1] In the 'Oxford' draft of 1922. Chapter III in current editions.

poems in *Minorities*, and more particularly the time at which they were copied out, show that the true continuity of his development was obscured in *Seven Pillars*. There are alternative biographical sources for this period, and these have provided a basis for the account which follows. Only this additional information and the inferences to be drawn from it make possible a clear understanding of the state of mind so strongly reflected in *Minorities*.

From what has already been said, it is clear that *Minorities* must not be read as 'autobiography', and that a 'biographical interpretation' cannot possibly be made by imposing ideas from the poems on to Lawrence's outlook. If his reasons for choosing many of the poems are to be understood, it is necessary to construct an entirely independent account of his thinking, derived from his own writings. A static account would be useless, since it would lead to false analogies between the poems and specific remarks; instead a coherent narrative is needed: describing the growth of particular ideas and their interrelationships. Beside such an account not only may the poems be seen to contain very real reflections of Lawrence's outlook, but also the ethos of the anthology is shown to belong to a defined period in his life, in which these opinions were in turn reached and left behind.

The study which follows makes no pretence to be biographically complete: limited space has precluded discussion even of several interesting facets of *Minorities*. There are also important differences between this account and conclusions reached by other biographical writers. These disagreements are not emphasized, since lengthy justification would distort the proportions of the narrative. Occasionally the presentation sacrifices strict chronology in order to follow the evolution of a particular idea, but since the passages quoted are dated, the relative time sequence is always available. Extensive use of quotation has had a number of drawbacks, especially in stylistic awkwardness, but I believe that this is outweighed by the authority of Lawrence's own words in such an essentially 'autobiographical' undertaking. Where I have summarized primary material, I have tried to present all aspects of the evidence fairly and without subjective intervention.

It seems to me wrong to speculate about links between individual poems and Lawrence's experience. Where there is direct evidence it is given in the Notes.

The poems in *Minorities* reflect the conclusion of Lawrence's first thirty years. Prominent themes in the anthology are nostalgia, and a sense of loss. By 1919, political entanglements barred him from the happiness of his life at Carchemish before the war, and death had taken the closest friends of his youth, among them his brother Will, killed in action in 1915. The last pre-war years, on which he now looked back, seem an appropriate biographical starting-point.

II.v.12
to his
mother,
H.L., p. 207 'You remember that passage [in C. M. Doughty's *Arabia Deserta*] that he who has once seen palm-trees and the goat-hair tents is never the same as he had been: that I feel very strongly, and I feel also that Doughty's two years wandering in untainted places made him the man he is, more than all his careful preparation before and since. My books would be the better, if I had been for a time in open country: and the Arab life is the only one that still holds the early poetry which is the easiest to read.'

Lawrence was twenty-two years old when he joined the British Museum excavations at Carchemish, a Hittite site near Jerablus on the Euphrates. The four years of archaeology which ended with the outbreak of the Great War were unquestionably the happiest in his life, and this extract from a letter written a few months later is one of many passages

24

testifying to the romantic idealism with which he viewed his surroundings: 'a wonderful place and time: as golden as Haroun al Raschid's in Tennyson'. In December 1913 he wrote to a friend: 'ever since knowing it I have felt that (at least for the near future) to talk of settling down to live in a small way anywhere else was beating the air ... I have got to like this place very much: and the people here – five or six of them – and the whole manner of living pleases me. We have 200 men to play with, anyhow we like so long as the excavations go on, and they are splendid fellows many of them ... and it is great fun with them. Then there are the digs, with dozens of wonderful things to find—it is like a great sport with tangible results at the end of things ... and hosts of beautiful things in the villages and towns to fill one's house with. Not to mention seal-hunting[1] in the country round about, and the Euphrates to rest in when one is over-hot. It is a place where one eats lotos nearly every day ...'

12.viii.27 to C. F. Shaw, B.M. 10.xii.13 to V. Richards, D.G., pp. 160–61

During these years at Carchemish, the first time he lived away from his parents' home, several of the qualities which contributed to his later outlook began to appear. His romantic reverence for medieval chivalry, and for the untainted Arab life, together with his idealization of art and craftsmanship, were a part of his rejection of contemporary values. Blackwood's *Centaur*, which he read in 1912, was 'very good, though not "all the way" enough for me: but at the same time more reasoned and definite as an attack on the modern world than anything I've read—bar Morris'.

6.i.12 to his mother, H.L., p. 184

This rejection expressed itself, then as later, in indifference towards money. 'Woolley [who took charge of the digs in 1912] has brought out a deal of money to speculate in antiquities: and he is in fair way of making about 300%. I am more modest, because I have still scruples about engaging in

2.x.12 to his mother, H.L., p. 235

[1] Hittite seals.

trade! Also I have little money to spend: somehow the temptation to make money is so very nauseous ...' He was paid 15 shillings a day for his work on the site: 'a very curious feeling: I don't like that also, but I felt incapable of refusing what will make me semi-independent'.

2.x.12
to his
mother
H.L., p. 235

There are already, in these early letters, intimations of the tensions in his personality which he later held responsible for many of the contradictions in his behaviour. Throughout his life opposing characteristics demanded satisfaction: the one through indulgence in luxury, and the other, much stronger, through Calvinistic austerity. Consequently, he was subject to dramatic conflicts which he is wrongly thought to have savoured for their own sake. In 1912, for example, he told his mother: 'after all, I feel very little lack of English scenery: we have too much greenery there, and one never feels the joy of a fertile place, as one does here when one finds a thorn-bush and green thistle. Here one learns an economy of beauty which is wonderful. England is fat—obese.'

12.ix.12
to his
mother,
H.L., p. 230

He had been brought up to regard undisciplined pleasure as sinful indulgence, and made a virtue of self-denial. Even at Oxford he held normal physical needs in wilful contempt, and at Carchemish he unwittingly trained himself for the immense hardships of his wartime role. A remark made in 1913, 'To escape the humiliation of loading in food, would bring one very near the angels', shows the extent to which self-denial had affected his values. In retrospect his brother A. W. Lawrence wrote: 'He had, I believe, a diffident, perhaps weak core, so controlled by his colossal will-power that its underlying presence was rarely suspected.' In 1925 Lawrence himself wrote: 'Garnett said once that I was two people, in my book:[1] one wanting to go on, the other wanting to go back. That is not right. Normally the very strong one, saying "No", the Puritan, is in firm charge, and the

15.vi.13
to his
mother,
H.L., p. 258

F., p. 590

28.ix.25
to C. F.
Shaw, B.M.

[1] *Seven Pillars of Wisdom.*

other poor little vicious fellow can't get a word in, for fear of him.' He attributed this conflict to characteristics inherited from his parents, but whilst for them there was a bond of affection which reconciled the warring elements and made them complementary, in himself the tension found no release. Lawrence returned to this subject repeatedly in his writings, and reached the conclusion (which is reflected in *Minorities*) that his birth had been a deep personal misfortune. The fear of passing on so great a source of misery was the reason he once gave for wanting no children of his own.

This notion of a struggle between two sides of his character seems to have been his only rationalization of 'the bundled powers and entities' that he recognized in his personality. Perhaps because he thought in these terms, the issues involved in his personal decisions became increasingly polarized: strength versus weakness; integrity versus dishonesty. S.P., Ch. CIII, p. 563

Such ideas evidently played a great part in his reactions towards sex. 'The lower creation I avoided, as an insult to our intellectual nature. If they forced themselves on me I hated them. To put my hand on a living thing was degradation to me: and it made me tremble if they touched me or took too quick an interest in me. This was an atomic repulsion, the power which guarded the intact course of a floating snowflake: but the opposite would have been my choice, if my head had not been tyrannous. I had a longing for women and animals, and lamented myself most when I saw a soldier hugging a girl in silent ecstasy, or a man fondling a dog: because my wish was to be as superficial, and my gaoler held me back.' S.P.(O), Ch. 118 (cf. S.P., Ch. CIII)

Like many Victorian children, he had been indoctrinated with ideas that the gratification of sexual desires was wicked, filthy, and perhaps dangerously unhealthy. He saw the reproductive process as 'an unhygienic pleasure', and drew S.P., Ch. LXI, p. 348

Mint, II,
Ch. 12,
p. 132

Mint, II,
Ch. 2,
p. 105

Ibid.

the conclusion that marriage merely gave the male 'a natural, cheap, sure and ready bed-partner'. In *The Mint* he recounted how 'At Oxford the select preacher, one evening service, speaking of venery, said "and let me implore you, my young friends, not to imperil your immortal souls upon a pleasure which, *so I am credibly informed*, lasts less than one and three-quarter minutes".' The many expressions of his views about sex leave no doubt that he had no experience whatsover of 'the perfect partnership, indulgence with a living body'. He continued to put forward his point of view with unshaken conviction, admitting only late in life the spiritual value of companionship in marriage. He then condemned the barren achievement of his uncorrupt celibacy which would lead in old age to misery. His innocence at the age of thirty can be accounted for by the circumstances of his life: his strict upbringing and the lack of feminine contact in his pre-war work. Later the lure of fame was to make all new friendships suspect, whilst the homosexual assault at Deraa in 1917 seems to have made him intensely mistrustful, as well as greatly strengthening his conviction that all sexual intimacies were selfish male impositions on an abused partner.

Minorities nevertheless contains several love poems, almost all of them retrospective. Just as he saw the years before the war as the happiest of his life, so he was afterwards convinced that they held his only experience of deep affection. He told Liddell Hart: 'One doesn't make real friends after twenty-five. The shell hardens', and wrote: 'People aren't friends till they have said all they can say, and are able to sit together, at work or rest, hour-long without speaking ... since S.A. died I haven't experienced any risk of that happening.' It was to 'S.A.' that he dedicated *Seven Pillars*, and these initials seem to have represented a composite idea. He told Liddell Hart that they stood for two different things. 'S' was a village in Syria, or property in it,

20.viii.33
B:L.H.,
p. 163

December
1923, to
R. A. Guy,
S.L., p. 163

1.viii.33
B:L.H.,
p. 143

and 'A' a person.[1] He once described the whole concept as 'an imaginary person of neutral sex'. More commonly, though, when he spoke of S.A. it was of 'a person, now dead, regard for whom lay beneath my labour for the Arabic peoples'. O.A., p. 26n 22.ix.23 to R. Buxton, D.G., p. 431

The dedicatory poem in *Seven Pillars* was a considerable achievement of literary synthesis. An outline drafted in 1919 reads: 'A(?). I wrought for him freedom to lighten his sad eyes: but he had died waiting for me. So I threw my gift away and now not anywhere will I find rest and peace.' The final version is Lawrence's only serious attempt to write poetry which has survived. The first of its four stanzas reads: 1919, S.T., 16.vi.68, p. 50, col. 1

I loved you, so I drew these tides of men into my hands S.P., p. 5
    and wrote my will across the sky in stars
To earn you Freedom, the seven pillared worthy house,
    that your eyes might be shining for me
                      When we came.

There is ample evidence that 'A', the personal element in this dedicatory poem, could only have been Dahoum, a headman at Carchemish, whose real name was Ahmed. He and Lawrence were close friends and tramped together through Syria between digging seasons. Dahoum went to England with another of the Arab headmen in 1913, and was on the expedition to Sinai in the following year. Judged by contemporary letters, their friendship was perfectly straightforward, though perhaps of a kind not previously experienced by Lawrence under the constraints of his family life. Dahoum was intelligent compared with the majority of village Arabs. He was good-looking, capable, and gifted with

---

[1] Lawrence made three statements confirming this, which override theories seeking to show that 'S' stands for a personal name, e.g. 'Sheik Ahmed' or 'Salim Ahmed'.

an irrepressible good humour which appealed strongly to Lawrence's own impish sense of fun.

There was, however, another aspect of the friendship, for it was through his Arab companions that Lawrence was able to discover the unspoiled peasant life he so revered. 'The perfectly hopeless vulgarity of the half-Europeanised Arab is appalling. Better a thousand times the Arab untouched. The foreigners come out here always to teach, whereas they had much better learn, for in everything but wits and knowledge the Arab is generally the better man of the two.'

Before the entry of Turkey into the Great War, Lawrence managed to arrange that Dahoum and the other headmen should perform their military service as official guards on the Carchemish site. In the late summer of 1918 Dahoum died of typhus; the tide of Arab Revolt was then still more than 200 miles to the south of Carchemish[1], and it is very improbable that the two had met since 1914.

Chief among Lawrence's motives in the Revolt was one which he described as 'personal': the gift of Arab freedom to S.A. This symbolic freedom was to protect the Arabs from foreign influence, especially the colonial ambitions of France. By the end of the Revolt the conscious motives that had drawn him into it were greatly magnified. Everywhere sensitive minds, surrounded by the unforeseen experiences and doubts of war, had fastened upon and intensified belief, drawing moral courage from simple, overmastering convictions of faith or loyalty.

It was probably this process, far more than any feelings he had experienced before the war, which made Lawrence believe that he had loved 'S.A.'. In 1924 when F. L. Lucas published 'Skias Onar' (No. 98) in the *New Statesman*,

---

[1] Lawrence told his younger brother after the war that Dahoum had died of typhus in 1918, still guarding the Carchemish site. Other evidence tends to confirm this.

Lawrence was deeply affected, especially by this last verse:

> So, love, I love not you but what I dream you,
>   My soul grows sick with clutching at a shade.
> Let others seem to win the shapes that seem you:
>   Only our pain is never masquerade.

The depression and self-condemnation reflected in *Minorities* had their origins in the central dilemma of his wartime role. In the original introductory chapter to *Seven Pillars* he wrote:

'The Cabinet raised the Arabs to fight for us by definite promises of self-government afterwards. Arabs believe in persons, not in institutions. They saw in me a free agent of the British Government, and demanded from me an endorsement of its written promises. So I had to join the conspiracy, and, for what my word was worth, assured the men of their reward. In our two years' partnership under fire they grew accustomed to believing me and to think my Government, like myself, sincere. In this hope they performed some fine things, but, of course, instead of being proud of what we did together, I was continually and bitterly ashamed.

'It was evident from the beginning that if we won the war these promises would be dead paper, and had I been an honest adviser of the Arabs I would have advised them to go home and not risk their lives fighting for such stuff: but I salved myself with the hope that, by leading these Arabs madly in the final victory, I would establish them, with arms in their hands, in a position so assured (if not dominant) that expediency would counsel to the Great Powers a fair settlement of their claims. In other words, I presumed (seeing no other leader with the will and power) that I would survive the campaigns, and be able to defeat not merely the Turks on the battlefield, but my own country and its allies

O.A., pp. 144–6

in the council-chamber. It was an immodest presumption: it is not yet clear if I succeeded:[1] but it is clear that I had no shadow of leave to engage the Arabs, unknowing, in such hazard. I risked the fraud, on my conviction that Arab help was necessary to our cheap and speedy victory in the East, and that better we win and break our word than lose.'

In this restrained statement he set down the appalling and inescapable moral impasse whose implications are not enlarged upon in *Seven Pillars*. Yet, very early in the Revolt, the horror of his position had begun to confront him and destroy his peace of mind. Contemporary evidence and the early 'Oxford' draft of *Seven Pillars* show that this is beyond doubt the 'personal tragedy' which he scaled down in the book.

In March 1917 he had put forward a new strategy for the Arabs, using their mobility to strike at Turkish supplies and tie down huge enemy contingents along the Hedjaz railway, yet carefully avoiding conventional battles and heavy casualties. For the execution of this strategy he needed the northern port of Akaba as base. At the beginning of May he set out with a small force on an immense inland loop, so as to capture, not merely the town, but the vital mountain passes behind it. On the way it was necessary to raise the local tribes, and in doing so he realized the gravity of his personal contribution to the fraud. In Chapter XLVIII of *Seven Pillars* he mentioned a long journey into Syria, to Damascus and beyond. The motive and military value of this expedition have been questioned, and some writers[2] doubt that it took place at all. Among his wartime notes, however, there is a contemporary draft message to General Clayton, heavily pencilled over. Under special

[1] Written in 1919.
[2] Despite the publication of an independent account, evidently based on Arab sources, in *The Arab Awakening* by George Antonius (Hamish Hamilton, London, 1938), pp. 221–2.

lighting and magnification it is possible to read the obliterated text:

'Clayton. I've decided to go off alone to Damascus, hoping to get killed on the way: for all sakes try and clear this show up before it goes further. We are calling them to fight for us on a lie, and I can't stand it.' B.M. (partly quoted S.L., p. 81)

Chapter 51 in the 'Oxford' draft of *Seven Pillars* contains an account of this incident so different from that in published editions that it seems worth quoting at length:

'... While I still saw the liberation of Syria happening in steps, of which Akaba was the indispensable first, I now saw the steps coming very close together, and ... planned to go off myself ... on a long tour of the north country to sound its opinion and learn enough to lay definite plans. My general knowledge of Syria was fairly good, and some parts I knew exactly: but I felt that one more sight of it would put straight the ideas of strategic geography given me by the Crusades and the first Arab conquest, and enable me to adjust them to the two new factors in my problem, the railways in Syria, and the allied army of Murray in Sinai. S.P.(O), Ch. 51

'Also I wanted an excuse to get away from the long guiding of people's minds and convictions which had been my part since Yenbo six months before. It should have been happiness, this lying out, free as air, with life about me striving its uttermost whither my own spirit led: but its unconscious serving of my purpose poisoned everything for me. A man might clearly destroy himself: but it was repugnant that the innocence and the ideals of the Arabs should enlist in my sordid service for me to destroy. We needed to win the war, and their inspiration had proved the best tool out here. The effort should have been its own reward:— might yet be, for the deceived:— but we the masters had promised them results in our false contract, and that was bargaining with life, a bluff in which we had nothing

33

wherewith to meet our stake. Inevitably we would reap bitterness, a sorry fruit of heroic endeavour.

'My ride was long and dangerous, no part of the machinery of the revolt, as barren of consequence as it was unworthy in motive. I met some of the more important of Feisal's secret friends, and saw the more important of our campaigning grounds: but it was artistically unjustifiable. At the time I was in reckless mood, not caring very much what I did, for in the journey up from Wejh I had convinced myself that I was the only person engaged in the field of the Arab adventure who could dispose it to be at once a handmaid to the British army of Egypt, and also at the same time the author of its own success.

'The abyss opened before me suddenly one night upon this ride, when in his tent old Nuri Shaalan bringing out his documents asked me bluntly which of the British promises were to be believed. I saw that with my answer I would gain or lose him: and in him the fortune of the Arab movement: and by my advice, that he should trust the latest in date of contradictory pledges, I passed definitely into the class of principal. In the Hedjaz the Sherifs were everything, and ourselves accessory: but in this distant north the repute of Mecca was low, and that of England very great. Our importance grew: our words were more weighty: indeed a year later I was almost the chief crook of our gang.

'So already I knew that when we had taken Akaba I would have to lead the movement, either directly or indirectly, and as I was little a man of action the prospect appeared hateful ... Accordingly on this march I took risks with the set hope of proving myself unworthy to be the Arab assurance of final victory. A bodily wound would have been a grateful vent for my internal perplexities, a mouth through which my troubles might have found relief.'

Biographers frequently attribute his later unhappiness to

the events at Deraa; but these occurred six months *later* than the Damascus journey. Clearly the 'rankling fraudulence' of his political role merits far more than a passing mention. *Seven Pillars* also contains many indirect reflections of this dilemma, such as the sophisticated ethical argument in Chapter C, and Lawrence's determination to avoid unnecessary Arab casualties: 'Throughout I tried to make the hurt of so exploiting the blood and hope of another people as small in degree as it seemed necessary in kind.' S.P., Ch. XC, p. 502 S.P.(O), Epilogue

In late January 1918 this humane principle was forgotten for a few hours in the Wadi Hesa, where he advised the Arabs to meet a Turkish force advancing on Tafileh. His later self-condemnation is bitterly spelled out: 'We had every advantage, of time, of terrain, of number, of weather, and could checkmate them easily: but to my wrath that was not enough. We would play their kind of game on our pigmy scale; deliver them a pitched battle such as they wanted; kill them all. I would rake up my memory of the half-forgotten maxims of the orthodox army text-book, and parody them in action. S.P., Ch. LXXXV, p. 476 25.i.18

'This was villainous, for with arithmetic and geography for allies we might have spared the suffering factor of humanity; and to make a conscious joke of victory was wanton. We could have won by refusing battle, foxed them by manoeuvring our centre as on twenty such occasions before and since: yet bad temper and conceit united for this time to make me not content to know my power, but determined to give public advertisement of it to the enemy and to everyone.'

The battle was, in Liddell Hart's words, 'a miniature masterpiece'—but Lawrence wrote that afterwards 'there was no glory left, but the terror of the broken flesh, which had been our own men, carried past us to their homes.' F., p. 183 S.P., Ch. LXXXVI, p. 482 25.1.18

He came to fear the exercise of authority which could so

S.P.
Ch. XC,
p. 502
21.ii.18

corrupt his judgment and degrade his personality: '... we glozed our fraud by conducting their necessary war purely and cheaply. But now this gloss had gone from me. Chargeable against my conceit were the causeless, ineffectual deaths of Hesa. My will had gone and I feared to be alone, lest the winds of circumstance, or power, or lust, blow my empty soul away.' In 1925, when he was revising this section of *Seven Pillars*, he wrote in a letter: 'So long as there is

28.ix.25
to C. F.
Shaw, B.M.

breath in my body my strength will be exerted to keep my soul in prison, since nowhere else can it exist in safety. The terror of being run away with, in the liberty of power, lies at the back of these many renunciations of my later life. I am afraid, of myself. Is this madness?'

By the end of the Desert War deeper knowledge of Arab character had destroyed his earlier reverence (though his love of the Arabian landscapes remained). In one post-war letter he condemned the idealized accounts so often given

17.vi.28
to C. F.
Shaw, B.M.

by casual European travellers in the Middle East: 'It just shows you how time and experience take the zest out of adventure. If I'd written the tale of my first travels in Syria, hunting Crusader Castles, I might have done this sort of thing. Indeed, I probably did it, cautiously, in letters home. Later I went to the very bottom of Arab life—and came back with the news that the seven pillars were fallen down.'

S.P.,
Ch. CVII,
p. 586
12.ix.18

By September 1918: 'I was tired to death of these Arabs; petty incarnate Semites who attained heights and depths beyond our reach, though not beyond our sight. They realized our absolute in their unrestrained capacity for good and evil; and for two years I had profitably shammed to be their companion!' The hint of simple poetry he had once seen in their lives was a reflection only of the empty desert. It was inseparable from their surroundings, and from the extreme and feckless conduct which desert living imposed on human behaviour.

Nevertheless his experience during these years alienated

him from European values. In July 1918 he wrote to Vyvyan Richards: 'You guessed rightly that the Arab appealed to my imagination. It is the old, old civilisation, which has refined itself clear of household gods, and half the trappings which ours hastens to assume. The gospel of bareness in materials is a good one, and it involves apparently a sort of moral bareness too. They think for the moment, and endeavour to slip through life without turning corners or climbing hills. In part it is a mental and moral fatigue, a race trained out, and to avoid difficulties they have to jettison so much that we think honourable and grave: and yet without in any way sharing their point of view, I think I can understand it enough to look at myself and other foreigners from their direction, and without condemning it. I know I'm a stranger to them, and always will be: but I cannot believe them worse, any more than I could change to their ways ... 15.vii.18 to V. Richards, D.G., p. 244

'Anyway these years of detachment have cured me from any desire ever to do anything for myself. When they untie my bonds I will not find in me any spur to action ... A house Ibid., p. 245 with no action entailed upon one, quiet, and liberty to think and abstain as one wills—yes, I think abstention, the leaving everything alone and watching the others still going past, is what I would choose today, if they ceased driving one ... A long quiet like a purge and then a contemplation Ibid., p. 246 and decision of future roads, that is what [there] is to look forward to.'

In *Seven Pillars* he returned to these ideas: 'In my case, the effort for these years to live in the dress of Arabs, and to imitate their mental foundation, quitted me of my English self, and let me look at the West and its conventions with new eyes: they destroyed it all for me. At the same time I could not sincerely take on the Arab skin: it was an affectation only. Easily was a man made an infidel, but hardly might he be converted to another faith. I had dropped one form and not taken on the other, and was become like S.P., Ch. I, pp. 31–2

Mohammed's coffin in our legend, with a resulting feeling of intense loneliness in life, and a contempt, not for other men, but for all they do.'

The capture of Damascus in October 1918 finally brought his personal predicament to a head. In the published *Seven Pillars*, though, it was the splendour of the occasion, and not his private misgivings, which he revealed: 'Every man, woman and child in this city of a quarter-million souls seemed in the streets, waiting only the spark of our appearance to ignite their spirits. Damascus went mad with joy. The men tossed up their tarbushes to cheer, the women tore off their veils. Householders threw flowers, hangings, carpets, into the road before us: their wives leaned, screaming with laughter, through the lattices and splashed us with bath-dippers of scent. ———

'Poor dervishes made themselves our running footmen in front and behind, howling and cutting themselves with frenzy; and over the local cries and the shrilling of women came the measured roar of men's voices, chanting, "Feisal, Nasir, Shukri, Urens" ...'

His romantic ambitions were now overwhelmingly fulfilled: 'I wanted to feel what it was like to be the mainspring of a national movement, and to have some millions of people expressing themselves through me: and being a half poet, I don't value material things much. Sensation and mind seem to me much greater, and the ideal, such a thing as the impulse that took us into Damascus, the only thing worth doing ...

'When I rode into Damascus the whole countryside was on fire with enthusiasm, and in the town a hundred thousand people shouted my name.' In a draft for the epilogue of *Seven Pillars* he wrote: 'From this cup I drank as deeply as any man should do, when we took Damascus: and was sated with it ...'

Yet the achievement was wholly superficial, for the

S.P.,
Ch. CXIX,
p. 646
1.x.18

14.xi.19
to C. J.
Kidston,
S.T.,
16.vi.68,
p. 49, col. 4

Ibid., col. 5

S.P.(O),
Epilogue

political battle still lay ahead. A paragraph in the 'Oxford' *Seven Pillars* describes his feelings on the evening of this triumphal entry to the town:

'I had been born free, and a stranger to those whom I had led for the two years, and to-night it seemed that I had given them all my gift, this false liberty drawn down to them by spells and wickedness, and nothing was left me but to go away. The dead army of my hopes, now turned to fact, confronted me, and my will, the worn instrument which had so long frayed our path, broke suddenly in my hand and fell useless. It told me that this Eastern chapter in my life was ended. There was the morrow and the next day of unrelenting care, that Feisal might surely gain the fruits of battle: and that was all my work.' S.P.(O), Ch. 137

At the Peace Conference Lawrence failed almost completely in his desperate ambition to obtain self-determination for the Arabs. His performance was astonishing; he put forward the Arab case with hypomanic powers of clarity and synthesis in argument and expression; but to no avail.

The extravagant pouring out of so much energy during these months, 'the worst I have lived through', could only lead to breakdown, since his nervous and physical resources were already overtaxed by the Revolt. During this time he also wrote the first draft of *Seven Pillars*, a constant reminder of the Arab sacrifice. Then, at the beginning of April, his father suddenly died of pneumonia, and only a few weeks later he himself was badly injured in an air crash. 18.x.27 to C.F. Shaw, B.M.

In August he returned to England, the chief agent, in his own eyes, in a successful fraud. He refused all honours, position or employment related to his wartime achievement, and retired to Oxford in a mood of bitter self-condemnation and disappointment. He was in a state of extreme depression and nervous exhaustion, and whilst Lowell Thomas lectured to packed houses about 'The Uncrowned King of Arabia', Lawrence drifted into deeper and

D.G.,
p. 294

deeper isolation. At home he would sit for an entire morning in the same position, without moving, and with the same expression on his face. The war had shattered the foundations of his self-respect, for the Arabs had trusted his word; he had witnessed their sacrifice; he knew the relatives of the dead.

For some months in 1919 and 1920 he lived at All Souls, where he had been elected to a research fellowship. A literary career now seemed the most attractive possibility open to him, and at All Souls he read widely among contemporary writers. Hoping to make *Seven Pillars* a classic of English literature, he struggled to improve his style, especially through a study of poetry for its imagery and economy of language.

Cf.
D.G., p. 360

The early poems in *Minorities* were copied out during this period of intense reading. This group includes not only the first thirteen poems, which came from scattered sources, but a series of twenty-four taken from *The Oxford Book of English Verse*, whose relevance to his predicament had probably attracted him before this.

He found it impossible to settle down at All Souls, and instead moved to London where solitary and spartan living suited his creative mood: literary success might provide a new basis for his self-respect. In March 1920 the French drove Feisal's Arab administration out of Damascus, making that year an even worse one for Lawrence than 1919. He was no longer officially connected with foreign policy, but he maintained through personal contacts and the press a continuous attack on the Middle Eastern settlement. The public interest aroused in England by Lowell Thomas proved an unexpected political asset, and Lawrence co-operated privately in the production of a series of articles. During 1920 the British Administration in Mesopotamia, target for many of his criticisms, became hopelessly embarrassed by local unrest and mounting military expense. In January 1921

Winston Churchill was appointed to the Colonial Office to find a solution. He persuaded Lawrence to join him as an expert adviser, and within a few months the Arabs were given recompense for their disappointments of 1919 and 1920. Afterwards Lawrence wrote: 'I ... must put on record my conviction that England is out of the Arab affair with clean hands.' But the move had come 'three years too late to earn the gratitude which peoples, if not states, can pay'.

18.xi.22
D.G.,
pp. 345–6
S.P.,
Ch. XLVIII,
p. 276n

He saw the settlement of 1921 as a greater achievement than all his earlier military and political successes; yet he continued to believe 'what I did in Arabia morally indefensible. So I ... will not take any personal profit out of it ... nor will I take any position which depends on my war-reputation.' The conviction that his wartime role had left an irredeemable moral stain remained unshaken.

10.viii.27
to R. Isham

There has been considerable confusion about Lawrence's contribution to Middle Eastern politics. His personal motives, policies and influence are frequently exaggerated or misunderstood. Particularly, there is no basis for the common assumption that his early sentiments towards the Arabs and against French colonization formed part of a sustained (uncritically Francophobic) policy afterwards evident at the Peace Conference. In each case his opinion had a specific and distinct cause. Before the war he believed that French Imperial practice—the imposition of French language, culture and social organization—would destroy the untainted Arab society he revered. Afterwards he opposed French ambitions in Syria because he had promised its government to Feisal in return for military help given to the Allies. In 1921 this promise was fulfilled in spirit when Britain gave Feisal Iraq instead, and Lawrence showed no special concern thereafter for the fate of northern Syria, whose population had not been greatly involved in the Revolt.

By 1922 popularity was proving far harder to bear than

political opposition. The achievement for which he was revered was repulsive to him, yet at every level in society he encountered inescapable and humiliating admiration. He was besieged by all kinds of hero hunters, especially women in search of a famous husband, and the tragically demented, who poured out their troubles to him in terrible letters. His reputation had become an unmitigated trial, and he determined that the time had come for 'Colonel Lawrence' to disappear. His distaste for public life had been confirmed by post-war visits to the Middle East on behalf of the Colonial Office: '... politics wearied me out, by worrying me overmuch. I've not got a coarse-fibred enough nature for them: and have too many scruples and an uneasy conscience. It's not good to see two sides of questions, when you have (officially) to follow one.' Early in 1922 he resigned.

13.vi.23
to D. G.
Hogarth,
D.G., p. 424

The third draft of *Seven Pillars* was now almost complete, but his optimism about its quality had begun to fade. In February he wrote: 'The real trouble is about my book, which is not good: not good enough to come out. It has grown too long and shapeless, and I haven't the strength to see it all in one piece, or the energy to tackle it properly. After I've got out of the Colonial Office and have been fallow for a time my interest in it will probably come back and then I'll have another go at it: but not at present.' Meanwhile he had a few copies printed in Oxford for private circulation among literary critics and his fellow officers in the Revolt; it is clear, though, that he never intended to publish this 'Oxford' draft.

16.ii.22
to E. H.
Kennington,
B.(R)

On July 20th, 1922, his letter of resignation appeared in the *Morning Post*. On the 21st the last eight chapters of *Seven Pillars* were delivered by the Oxford printer. The completion of this 330,000-word draft had left him completely exhausted—'I nearly went off my head in London this spring, heaving at that beastly book of mine'—but now at last he was free of all outward commitments.

12.xi.22
to R.
Graves,
B:R.G.,
p. 23

There is no reason to doubt his statement that he had decided to enlist in 1919, 'but not till Winston had given the Arabs a fair deal was I free to please myself. That accounted for the delay till 1922.' In the later stages of the desert campaign he had occasionally worked with regular British units, and he said that 'these friendly outings with the armoured car and Air Force fellows were what persuaded me that my best future, if I survived the war, was to enlist.'

July 1927 to R. Graves, B:R.G., p. 77

August 1927, B:R.G., p. 95

There is clear evidence that his decision was linked with his wartime experience and conclusions. He wrote to Lionel Curtis: 'on my last night in Barton Street I read Chapters 113–118 [the introspective central section of Book IX in the 'Oxford' draft[1]] and saw implicit in them my late course.' In the last of these chapters he had written: 'There seemed a level of certainty in degradation, a final safety. Man could rise to any height, but there was an animal point beneath which he could not fall. It was a solid satisfaction on which to rest.' A letter to Robert Graves referring to the same occasion, is more detailed: 'Honestly I couldn't tell you exactly why I joined up: though the night before I did (a very wonderful night by the way: I felt like a criminal waiting for daylight) I sat up and wrote out all the reasons I could see or feel in myself for it. But they came to little more than that it was a necessary step, forced on me by an inclination towards ground-level: by a despairing hope that I'd find myself on common ground with men: by a little wish to make myself a little more human than I had become in Barton Street: by an itch to make myself ordinary in a mob of likes: also I'm broke, so far as money goes ... All these are reasons: but unless they are cumulative they are miserably inadequate. I wanted to join up, that's all: and I am still glad, sometimes, that I did. It's going to be a brain-sleep, and I'll come out of it less odd than I went in: or at least less odd in other men's eyes.'

19.iii.23 to L. Curtis, D.G., p. 411

S.P.(O), Ch. 118

12.xi.22 to R. Graves, B:R.G., p. 23

[1] Chapter XCIX to CIII in current editions.

43

As 352087 A/C Ross, Lawrence was able to take very few personal possessions to the R.A.F. training depot, but *Minorities* was among them. The anthology seems to have grown little during the previous two years of hectic activity; now, however, he copied out a second large group of poems to which he added steadily until late 1923, when the notebook was about three-quarters filled.

12.xi.22
to W.
Rothenstein,
B.(R)/H.

Three months after enlisting he wrote: 'I've shut myself up ... and intend to be a hermit till I have accomplished what lies in my mind: or till I give up trying it.' In *The Mint*, which is based on notes made during his training, he described in bitter detail the severe, sometimes inhuman, treatment meted out to recruits. This was a strong challenge to his 'determined endeavour ... to scrape through with it, into the well-paid peace of my trade as photographer to some squadron. To that I look forward as profession and livelihood for many years: — for good, I hope, since the stresses of my past existence give me warrant, surely, for thinking that my course will not be too long. How welcome is death, someone said, to them that have nothing to do but to die.

Mint, I,
Ch. 25,
pp. 86–7

'Meanwhile there is this training to be gone through, desperately, with my refuge at stake. Half a dozen times I have nearly cracked: but not very lately. Every week things seem easier.'

At the end of 1922 sudden newspaper exposure caused Lawrence to be discharged, but by then no other life would satisfy him: 'for at Farnborough I grew suddenly on fire with the glory which the air should be ...' He re-enlisted almost at once, in the Tank Corps, and served for nearly two and a half years as Pte. T. E. Shaw at Bovington Camp, in Dorset. But army life proved no substitute for the Air Force, which had offered him an opportunity to regain his self-respect through individual excellence. 'In the army the person is at a discount: the combined movement, the body

19.iii.23
to L. Curtis,
D.G., p. 411

1927,
B:R.G.,
pp. 53 and
123

of men, is the ideal. In the R.A.F. there are no combined movements.' He described the ideal aircraftman as 'the skilled individual mechanic at his bench or machine. Our job is the conquest of the air, our element.'

Despite the friendships he made at Bovington there was little to halt the erosion of his morale. In May 1923 he wrote: 'When I embarked on it, a year ago ... I thought it a mood, and curable: while today I feel that there is no change before me, and no hope of change.' By September: 'my thoughts are centring more and more upon the peace of death, with longing for it. Is it, do you think, that at last I am getting old? Do old people secretly dwell much upon their inevitable end?' 20.v.23 to L. Curtis D.G., p. 418

25.ix.23 to L. Curtis, All Souls

It is probably more than a coincidence that a number of his friends, including D. G. Hogarth and Lionel Curtis (recipient of the above remarks), began that autumn to press for a revised subscription issue of *Seven Pillars*. The details were finally settled in early December. Lawrence had already returned to writing in the summer, when he translated *Le Gigantesque* by Adrien Le Corbeau.[1] Both in his letters and in *Minorities* there is a distinct pastoral note at this time. His ideas about literary style were also changing. In October 1923 he wrote: 'Do you know that lately I have been finding my deepest satisfaction in the collocation of words so ordinary and plain that they cannot mean anything to a book-jaded mind: and out of some of such I can draw deep stuff. Is it perhaps that certain sequences of vowels or consonants imply more than others: that writing of this sort has music in it? I don't want to affirm it, and yet I would not deny it: for if writing can have sense (and it has: this letter has) and sound why shouldn't it have something of pattern too? My sequences seem to be independent of ear ... to impose themselves through the eye alone. I achieved a good many of them in *Le Gigantesque*: but fortuitously for 4.x.23 to E. Garnett, D.G., pp. 433-4

[1] *The Forest Giant* (Cape, London, 1924).

45

2.iv.28
to H.
Williamson,
H.W., p. 20

the most part.' His own book proved to be a depressing factor. 'I'll never forget the despair', he wrote later, 'with which I read my *Seven Pillars* in 1923, after forgetting it for two years. It was incredibly unlike what I'd thought my talents (of which I'd had too good an opinion) would bring forth ...' Work on the edition was to drag on for three years, while he revised the text sentence by sentence.

In June 1925 he gave way suddenly to despair. Repeated requests for transfer back to the Air Force had all failed, and he could see no purpose in life beyond the completion of *Seven Pillars*. Sending his revised draft of Book VI (the emotional nadir of the work) to Edward Garnett, he wrote:

13.vi.25
to E.
Garnett,
D.G.,
pp. 476–7

'What muck, irredeemable, irremediable, the whole thing is! How on earth can you have once thought it passable? My gloomy view of it deepens each time I have to wade through it. If you want to see how good situations, good characters, good material can be wickedly bungled, refer to any page, passim. There isn't a scribbler in Fleet Street who wouldn't have got more fire and colour into every paragraph.

'Trenchard withdrew his objection to my rejoining the Air Force. I got seventh-heaven for two weeks: but then Sam Hoare came back from Mespot and refused to entertain the idea. That, and the closer acquaintance with *The Seven Pillars* (which I now know better than anyone ever will) have together convinced me that I'm no bloody good on earth. So I'm going to quit: but in my usual comic fashion I'm going to finish the reprint and square up with Cape before I hop it! There is nothing like deliberation, order and regularity in these things.

'I shall bequeath you my notes on life in the recruits camp of the R.A.F.[1] They will disappoint you.'

Hoare's objections were hastily overruled through the intervention of the Prime Minister, and in August Lawrence

---

[1] Later re-arranged and edited to form the first two sections of *The Mint*.

once more became an aircraftman, at Cranwell. This transfer marks the starting point of the final, increasingly contented period in his working life. The early problems of 'fitting in' were long past, and he no longer found it necessary to hide his past identity. He was neither like the other men, nor uncomfortably different from them, but on the basis of mutual respect he lived among them easily. His self-confidence grew, though it was still vulnerable. Perhaps the bitterest of all his letters was written a few weeks after the move to Cranwell, following an ill-judged visit to London to meet Winterton and Feisal: 'Winterton of course had to talk of old times, taking me for a companion of his again, as though we were again advancing on Damascus. And I had to talk back, keeping my end up, as though the R.A.F. clothes were a skin that I could slough off at any while with a laugh.

28.ix.25 to C. F. Shaw, B.M.

'But all the while I knew I couldn't ... My reason tells me all the while, dins into me day and night, a sense of how I've crashed my life and self and gone hopelessly wrong: and hopelessly it is, for I'm never coming back, and I want to.'

In December 1926 he was posted to Karachi. 'It is a misery and shame', he wrote of himself to a Cranwell friend, 'being here again in this East where he did so blacken his character in 1917 and 1918, and he skulks among the airmen out of sight, very remorseful.' Two weeks later he told Charlotte Shaw that 'The Depot is dreary, to a degree, and its background makes me shiver. It is a desert, very like Arabia: and all sorts of haunting likenesses (pack-donkeys, the colour and cut of men's clothes, an oleander bush in flower in the valley, camel-saddles, tamarisk) try to remind me of what I've been for eight years desperately fighting out of my mind. Even I began to doubt if the coming out here was wise. However there wasn't much chance, and it must be made to do. It will do, as a matter of fact, easily.'

11.i.27 to J. S. Hollings, B.

28.i.27 to C. F. Shaw, B.M.

The 'special note' of *Minorities* was out of sympathy with his contented life at Cranwell, described in the final section of *The Mint*, and he does not seem to have added to the anthology during those sixteen months. He was frequently sent books by literary friends, and now formed a small library, used by the airmen, on each successive station. Consequently his dependence on *Minorities* diminished, but when he sailed to India he could pack only a few of his Cranwell books for forwarding, and in January 1927 he wrote asking that these be 're-packed in thick paper marked "second hand" and ... their value, for customs purposes, be assessed at not more than 6/– per parcel. This worm has to pay duty ...' Included among them were *Minorities* and a notebook which probably contained the jottings for *The Mint*.

11.i.27 to J. S. Hollings, B.

After the first few weeks at Karachi he was given absorbing and satisfying duties. Until then, though, he was unhappy, and near the end of *Minorities* a few poems echo this feeling. Nevertheless, by the end of that year his self-confidence had overcome the outlook predominant in the anthology, and there can be little doubt that he gave it away in November knowing that it was no longer relevant to his state of mind. His letter to Mrs Shaw states that he had copied the poems into another notebook before sending her the original. This remark may have been a fiction intended to suggest that he had not deprived himself, since I have found no reference to a later anthology, and doubt that many of these poems would have held a special appeal during the last years of his life.

17.xi.27

At no later time do his letters convey the acute recrimination and mental suffering evident in the seven post-war years. Whatever his convictions about the past, their hold over his emotions faded. He came to see *Seven Pillars* as 'the self-argument of a man who couldn't then see straight: and who now thinks that perhaps it did not matter: that seeing straight is only an illusion. We do these things in

15.v.30 to F. Manning, D.G., p. 692

48

sheer vapidity of mind, not deliberately, not consciously even. To make out that we were reasoned cool minds, ruling our courses and contemporaries, is a vanity. Things happen, and we do our best to keep in the saddle.' In May 1928 he wrote: 'The causes that led me into the Air Force have come to their full consequence, and are dead, like the Arab business, probably: at least I have felt strong enough to put them out on paper ...' He remained in the R.A.F. 'because I like it. That wasn't the reason of my joining up: but after I'd been six months in the ranks, and had got used to the discomforts of rough living and of being chased about by all manner of silly people, I found that it was a life which suited me exactly: and if I could be always healthy I'd wish to keep in it for ever: but at home! Bother these overseas places! No fun for troops out here.' Bodily servitude and the renunciation of authority had left his mind free from demands of self-preservation or responsibility: 'the army leaves you all your thinking-time to yourself,' he had written in 1923. Even in moments of depression he was confident that his course was right: 'The Scotch talk about "dreeing one's weird", I dree mine: and there cannot be anything to regret. The machine runs at full speed every day, and no one ... dare say that it's running in the wrong direction.'

17.v.28 to C. F. Shaw, B.M.

18.vi.27 to J. F. Allanson, *Birmingham Evening Mail*, 27.ix.62

12.v.23 to A. R. D. Fairburn, A.T.

27.xi.28 to C. F. Shaw, B.M.

The remarkable recovery of his self-possession, and his enthusiasm for work on high-speed craft between 1929 and 1935 belong to a later period than *Minorities*, and prove that the anthology can be related only to the time in which it was compiled. During his last years Lawrence's talents were once more applied to constructive achievement, and his outlook changed greatly. In December 1930 he wrote: 'I have nearly finished the Greek,[1] and it has been a quiet year, of no publicity at all. This has been the first year for ten years to leave me quite at peace. I think that is very good. One

5.xii.30 to C. F. Shaw, B.M.

[1] His translation of *The Odyssey*.

or two more, and my existence will be taken for granted.'
Three and a half years later, whilst giving advice to a young
poet, he wrote what can only be seen as a rejection of much
of the sentiment embodied in *Minorities*:

18.v.34
to R. M.
Gouldby, B.

'... you ... feel eloquently about old age and death, and
the movements of time. Most people do feel these things,
and some few are eloquent upon them. Those that can be
eloquent upon them—or moving, which perhaps is closer
to what I mean—achieve their best eloquence (their only
eloquence, often)—upon these time themes. You are defi-
nitely good—very good indeed—in some of these yearnings
and grievous lines.

'Yet I will beg you not to be too pleased with that. The
very young often are half in love with Death—and half
afraid of him. Later, when Death is nearer, you will be
reluctant to think so closely of him. Nor is a sorrowful
mood much provision for a life of letters.'

Exactly a year later, Lawrence died in Bovington Military
Hospital.

J. M. WILSON

Note on Contents

In the manuscript of *Minorities* neither the titles of the poems nor the names of the poets are given. For this edition Lawrence's scheme has been preserved, except that the poems are numbered for reference to the list of poems opposite and the notes following the text. There is no evidence that he had made any similar personal anthology before this one, but during the later Arab campaigns he had carried with him the *The Oxford Book of English Verse* (*O.E.V.*). A large proportion of the early poems in *Minorities* also appear in the Oxford anthology. The list of poems names collections of poetry found after Lawrence's death in the Clouds Hill library or mentioned in letters, from which he probably took the poems; where these were inscribed 'T.E.L.', it is reasonable to assume that he acquired them before his enlistment in 1922. No collection is named where there are several equally possible sources.

Nine poems written in Lawrence's own hand are reproduced in facsimile next to the relevant typeset verses.

List of Poems

9 William Morris
from 'The Story of the Glittering Plain'
The Story of the Glittering Plain (London, 1904). 'T.E.L.'

10 William Morris
from 'Spell-bound'
The Defence of Guenevere and other Poems

11 W. E. Henley
'Hawthorn and Lavender' XLIX
Hawthorn and Lavender, with other Verses (London, 1901).
'T.E.L.'

12 James Elroy Flecker
'The Pensive Prisoner'
The Collected Poems of James Elroy Flecker, with an Intro-
duction by J. C. Squire (4th impression, London, 1918).
'T.E.L. 1919 Paris'

13 Johann Wolfgang von Goethe
from *Faust*, Act I, Scene 1
Faust, 2 vols (London, 1906–10). Vol. I: 'J.H.R.'. Vol. II:
'T.E.S.'

14 Ernest Dowson
'Vesperal'
The Poems of Ernest Dowson, with a Memoir by Arthur
Symons (London, 1913). 'T.E.L.'

15 Algernon Swinburne
from a chorus in *Atalanta in Calydon*
Atalanta in Calydon: a tragedy (London, 1894). 'T.E.L.
1920'

16 Henry Cust
'Non Nobis'
O.E.V.

17 John Donne
'A Hymn to God the Father'
O.E.V.

28 William Wordsworth
from 'Poems of Sentiment and Reflection', XLII
Poetical Works, ed. T. Hutchinson (London, 1917).
'T.E.L.'

29 Edward Thomas
'The Owl'
Collected Poems, with a Foreword by Walter de la Mare
(London, 1920). 'T.E.L.'

30 R. D. Blackmore
'Dominus Illuminatio Mea'
O.E.V.

31 William Wordsworth
from 'Ode: Intimations of Immortality from Recollec-
tions of Early Childhood'
O.E.V.

32 T. E. Brown
'Salve!'
O.E.V.

33 Sir Henry Wotton
from 'Elizabeth of Bohemia'
O.E.V.

34 George Herbert
'Love'
O.E.V.

35 Sir William Watson
'The Great Misgiving'
O.E.V.

36 Samuel Taylor Coleridge
from 'Youth and Age'
O.E.V.

37 James Shirley
'Death the Leveller'
O.E.V.

38 James Thompson ('B.V.')
'The Vine' ('Sunday up the River', XVIII)
O.E.V.

39 James Thompson ('B.V.')
'Sunday up the River', XVI
The City of Dreadful Night, and other poems (London,
1910).

40 Christina Rossetti
from 'Bride Song'
O.E.V.

41 Samuel Taylor Coleridge
'Kubla Khan'
O.E.V.

42 Siegfried Sassoon
'Everyone Sang'
Picture Show (Cambridge, 1919). 'T.E.L.'

43 John Keats
'Ode to a Nightingale'
O.E.V.

44 Siegfried Sassoon
'Limitations'
from a manuscript fair copy by Sassoon written for
Lawrence into *Picture Show* in December 1919

45 Ralph Hodgson
'Eve'
Poems (London, 1917). 'T.E.L. Cairo 1917'

46 Siegfried Sassoon
'Memory'
Picture Show (Cambridge, 1919). 'T.E.L.'

47 Siegfried Sassoon
'The Dug-Out'
Picture Show (Cambridge, 1919). 'T.E.L.'

48 D. G. Rossetti
'Sunset Wings'
Sonnets and Lyrical Poems (London, 1894). 'T.E.L.'

49 Ralph Hodgson
'The Mystery'
Poems (London, 1917). 'T.E.L. Cairo 1917'

50 Thomas Lovell Beddoes
'Dream-Pedlary'
[Lawrence's MS. differs from *O.E.V.*]

51 Anon (Christ Church MS.)
'Preparations'
O.E.V.

52 Arthur Hugh Clough
'Say not the Struggle Naught availeth'
O.E.V.

53 James Thomson ('B.V.')
'Sunday up the River', XVII
The City of Dreadful Night and other poems (London, 1910)

54 D. G. Rossetti
from 'The Cloud confines'
Sonnets and Lyrical Poems (London, 1894). 'T.E.L.'

55 James Thomson ('B.V.')
'Sunday up the River', I
The City of Dreadful Night and other poems (London, 1910)

56 Algernon Swinburne
'The Oblation'
Songs before Sunrise (London, 1909). 'T.E.L. 1919'

57 Ralph Hodgson
'The Moor'
Poems (London, 1917). 'T.E.L. Cairo 1917'

58 James Thomson ('B.V.')
'A Song of Sighing'
The City of Dreadful Night and other poems (London, 1910)

59 D. G. Rossetti
from 'Youth and Lordship'
Sonnets and Lyrical Poems (London, 1894). 'T.E.L.'

60 James Thomson ('B.V.')
'Day'
The City of Dreadful Night and other poems (London, 1910)

61 Algernon Swinburne
'The Pilgrims'
Songs before Sunrise (London, 1909). 'T.E.L. 1919'

62 Matthew Arnold
'Self-dependence'

63 D. G. Rossetti
'A little while'
Sonnets and Lyrical Poems (London, 1894). 'T.E.L.'

64 James Thomson ('B.V.')
'Song'
The City of Dreadful Night and other poems (London, 1910)

65 John Davidson
from 'The Last Journey', epilogue to
The Testament of John Davidson (London, 1908). 'T.E.L.'

66 Percy Bysshe Shelley
from 'Prometheus Unbound', Act IV
The Poetical Works (London, 1895). 'T.E.L.'

67 A. E. Housman
'Epitaph on an Army of Mercenaries'
Last Poems (London, 1922)

68 A. E. Housman
'Eight O'clock'
Last Poems (London, 1922)

69 D. G. Rossetti
'The Blessed Damozel'
O.E.V.

70 Algernon Swinburne
'Super Flumina Babylonis'
Songs before Sunrise (London, 1909). 'T.E.L. 1919'

71 John Davidson
'In Romney Marsh'
Ballads and Songs (London, 1894)

72 Percy Bysshe Shelley
from 'Hellas'
The Poetical Works (London, 1895). 'T.E.L.' Also in
O.E.V.

73 A. E. Housman
'Revolution'
Last Poems (London, 1922)

74 Percy Bysshe Shelley
from 'Stanzas written in dejection, near Naples'
The Poetical Works (London, 1895). 'T.E.L.'

75 D. G. Rossetti
'The Staff and Scrip'
Ballads and Narrative Poems (London, 1893). 'T.E.L.'

76 John Davidson
from 'Spring'
Ballads and Songs (London, 1894)

77 Percy Bysshe Shelley
'The Cloud'
The Poetical Works (London, 1895). 'T.E.L.'

78 John Crowe Ransom
'The Lover'
Poems about God (New York, 1919)

79 James Elroy Flecker
'Stillness'
The Collected Poems of James Elroy Flecker, with an Intro-
duction by J. C. Squire (4th impression, London, 1918).
'T.E.L. 1919 Paris'

80 W. B. Yeats
'A Faery Song'
Poems (reprint of 3rd edn, London, 1913). 'T.E.L.'

81 Edward Thomas
'The New House'
Collected Poems, with a Foreword by Walter de la Mare
(London, 1920). 'T.E.L.'

82 Thomas Hardy
'To the Moon'
Moments of Vision

83 Walter de la Mare
'Arabia'
The Listeners and others poems (4th impression, London,
1918). 'T.E.L. 1919'

84 Charles Hamilton Sorley
'The Song of the Ungirt Runners'
Marlborough and other poems (Cambridge, 1919). 'T.E.L.'

85 W. B. Yeats
'The Lake Isle of Innisfree'
Poems (reprint of 3rd edn, London, 1913). 'T.E.L.'

86 Robert Graves
'A Forced Music'
Whipperginny (London, 1923). Presentation copy from
the author signed 17.iii.1923

87 William Morris
from 'Sir Galahad: a Christmas Mystery'
The Defence of Guenevere and other poems

88 Thomas Hardy
'When I set out for Lyonnesse'
Satires of Circumstance: Lyrics and Reveries (London, 1915).
'T.E.L.'

89 Joseph Blanco White
from the sonnet 'Night and Death'

90 Alice Meynell
'Parentage'
The Poems of Alice Meynell: Complete Edition (London, 1923)

91 William Blake
'Song'
Poetical Sketches (n.pl., Ballantyne Press, 1899). 'T.E.L.'

92 William Morris
'The Nymph's Song to Hylas'
O.E.V.

93 Thomas Hardy
'The Ivy-Wife'
Wessex Poems and other verses

94 William Blake
'Jerusalem' from *Milton*
Milton, ed. E. R. D. Maclagan and A. G. B. Russell (London, 1907), 'T.E.L.'

95 Sir Walter Raleigh
'His Pilgrimage'
O.E.V.

96 William Morris
from 'The Wind'
The Defence of Guenevere and other poems

97 Thomas Hardy
final chorus from *The Dynasts*
The Dynasts (London, 1923, 1924)

98 F. L. Lucas
'Skias Onar'
The *New Statesman*, 9.viii.1924. A revised version of this poem was published under the title 'Envoi' in *Time and Memory* (London, 1929)

99 James Stephens
'The Snare'

100 Walter de la Mare
'The Song of Shadows'
Peacock Pie: a book of rhymes (5th impression, London, 1919). 'T.E.L. 1919'

101 Hilaire Belloc
from 'Stanzas written on Battersea Bridge during a South-Westerly Gale'
Verses (new edn, London, 1911). 'T.E.S.'

102 Edward Thomas
'Lights Out'
Collected Poems, with a Foreword by Walter de la Mare (London, 1920). 'T.E.L.'

103 William Morris
'The Judgment of God'
The Defence of Guenevere and other poems

104 Thomas Hardy
'The Impercipient: (At a Cathedral Service)'
Wessex Poems and other verses

105 Alice Meynell
'Via, et Veritas, et Vita'
The Poems of Alice Meynell: Complete Edition (London, 1923)

106 Alice Meynell
' "I am the Way" '
The Poems of Alice Meynell: Complete Edition (London, 1923)

107 William Morris
from 'The Defence of Guenevere'
The Defence of Guenevere and other poems

108 Humbert Wolfe
'The Harlot', I
Requiem (London, 1927)

109 William Blake
'I fear'd the fury of my wind'
Poetry and Prose, ed. G. Keynes (London, 1927). Presentation copy from the editor dated August 1927

110 William Shakespeare
from *Hamlet*, Act IV, Scene 5
Works, ed. W. J. Craig (Oxford, 1892). Sent to India by J. S. Hollings in January 1927

111 William Blake
'Mad Song'
Poetry and Prose, ed. G. Keynes (London, 1927). Presentation copy from the editor dated August 1927

112 William Morris
from 'The Hollow Land'

MINORITIES

I

We who with songs beguile your pilgrimage
    And swear that Beauty lives though lilies die,
We Poets of the proud old lineage
    Who sing to find your hearts, we know not why,—

What shall we tell you? Tales, marvellous tales
    Of ships and stars and isles where good men rest,
Where nevermore the rose of sunset pales,
    And winds and shadows fall toward the West:

And there the world's first huge white-bearded kings
    In dim glades sleeping, murmur in their sleep,
And closer round their breasts the ivy clings,
    Cutting its pathway slow and red and deep.

.   .   .   .   .

And how beguile you? Death has no repose
    Warmer and deeper than that Orient sand
Which hides the beauty and bright faith of those
    Who made the Golden Journey to Samarkand.

And now they wait and whiten peaceably,
    Those conquerors, those poets, those so fair:
They know time comes, not only you and I,
    But the whole world shall whiten, here or there;

When those long caravans that cross the plain
    With dauntless feet and sound of silver bells
Put forth no more for glory or for gain,
    Take no more solace from the palm-girt wells.

When the great markets by the sea shut fast
  All that calm Sunday that goes on and on:
When even lovers find their peace at last,
  And Earth is but a star, that once had shone.

2

I

Upon her plodding palfrey
With a heavy child at her breast
And Joseph holding the bridle
They mount to the last hill-crest.

Dissatisfied and weary
She sees the blade of the sea
Dividing earth and heaven
In a glitter of ecstasy.

Sudden a dark-faced stranger
With his back to the sun, holds out
His arms; so she lights from her palfrey
And turns her round about.

She has given the child to Joseph,
Gone down to the flashing shore;
And Joseph, shading his eyes with his hand,
Stands watching evermore.

II

The sea in the stones is singing,
A woman binds her hair
With yellow, frail sea-poppies,
That shine as her fingers stir.

While a naked man comes swiftly
Like a spurt of white foam rent
From the crest of a falling breaker,
Over the poppies sent.

He put his surf-wet fingers
Over her startled eyes,
And asks if she sees the land, the land,
The land of her glad surmise.

III

Again in her blue, blue mantle
Riding at Joseph's side,
She says, 'I went to Cythera,
And woe betide!'

Her heart is a swinging cradle
That holds the perfect child,
But the shade on her forehead ill becomes
A mother mild.

So on with the slow, mean journey
In the pride of humility;
Till they halt at a cliff on the edge of the land
Over a sullen sea.

While Joseph pitches the sleep-tent
She goes far down to the shore
To where a man in a heaving boat
Waits with a lifted oar.

IV

They dwelt in a huge, hoarse sea-cave
And looked far down the dark
Where an archway torn and glittering
Shone like a huge sea-spark.

He said: 'Do you see the spirits
Crowding the bright doorway?'
He said: 'Do you hear them whispering?'
He said: 'Do you catch what they say?'

V

Then Joseph, grey with waiting,
His dark eyes full of pain,
Heard: 'I have been to Patmos;
Give me the child again.'

Now on with the hopeless journey
Looking bleak ahead she rode,
And the man and the child of no more account
Than the earth the palfrey trode.

Till a beggar spoke to Joseph,
But looked into her eyes;
So she turned, and said to her husband:
'I give, whoever denies.'

VI

She gave on the open heather
Beneath bare judgment stars,
And she dreamed of her children and Joseph,
And the isles, and her men, and her scars.

And she woke to distil the berries
The beggar had gathered at night,
Whence he drew the curious liquors
He held in delight.

He gave her no crown of flowers,
No child and no palfrey slow,
Only led her through harsh, hard places
Where strange winds blow.

She follows his restless wanderings
Till night when, by the fire's red stain,
Her face is bent in the bitter steam
That comes from the flowers of pain.

Then merciless and ruthless
He takes the flame-wild drops
To the town, and tries to sell them
With the market-crops.

So she follows the cruel journey
That ends not anywhere,
And dreams, as she stirs the mixing-pot,
She is brewing hope from despair.

3

'No one care less than I,
Nobody knows but God,
Whether I am destined to lie
Under a foreign clod,'
Were the words I made to the bugle call in the morning.

But laughing, storming, scorning,
Only the bugles know
What the bugles say in the morning,
And they do not care, when they blow
The call that I heard and made words to early this morning.

4

They are not long, the weeping and the laughter,
  Love and desire and hate:
I think they have no portion in us after
    We pass the gate.

They are not long, the days of wine and roses:
  Out of a misty dream
Our path emerges for a while, then closes
    Within a dream.

They are not long, the weeping and the laughter,
  Love and desire and hate:
I think they have no portion in us after
    We pass the gate.

They are not long, the days of wine and roses:
  Out of a misty dream
Our path emerges for a while, then closes
    Within a dream.

5

Does the road wind uphill all the way?
   Yes, to the very end.
Will the day's journey take the whole long day?
   From morn to night, my friend.

But is there for the night a resting-place?
   A roof for when the slow, dark hours begin.
May not the darkness hide it from my face?
   You cannot miss that inn.

Shall I meet other wayfarers at night?
   Those who have gone before.
Then must I knock, or call when just in sight?
   They will not keep you waiting at that door.

Shall I find comfort, travel-sore and weak?
   Of labour you shall find the sum.
Will there be beds for me and all who seek?
   Yea, beds for all who come.

6

When you are dead, when all you could not do
   Leaves quiet the worn hands, the weary head,
Asking not any service more of you,
   Requiting you with peace when you are dead;

When, like a robe, you lay your body by,
   Unloosed at last,—how worn, and soiled, and frayed!—
Is it not pleasant just to let it lie
   Unused and be moth-eaten in the shade?

Folding earth's silence round you like a shroud,
   Will you just know that what you have is best:—
Thus to have slipt unfamous from the crowd;
   Thus having failed and failed, to be at rest?

O, having, not to know! Yet O, my Dear,
   Since to be quit of self is to be blest;
To cheat the world, and leave no imprint here,—
   Is this not best?

7

How splendid in the morning glows the lily: with what
    grace he throws
His supplication to the rose: do roses nod the head, Yasmin?

But when the silver dove descends I find the little flower of
    friends
Whose very name that sweetly ends I say when I have said,
    Yasmin.

The morning light is clear and cold: I dare not in that light
    behold
A whiter light, a deeper gold, a glory too far shed, Yasmin.

But when the deep red eye of day is level with the lone
    highway,
And some to Meccah turn to pray, and I toward thy bed,
    Yasmin;

Or when the wind beneath the moon is drifting like a soul
    aswoon,
And harping planets talk love's tune with milky wings
    outspread, Yasmin,

Shower down thy love, O burning bright! For one night
    or the other night
Will come the Gardener in white, and gathered flowers are
    dead, Yasmin.

8

Before my light goes out for ever if God should give me a
    choice of graces,
    I would not reck of length of days, nor crave for things to
      be;
But cry: 'One day of the great lost days, one face of all the
    faces,
    Grant me to see and touch once more and nothing more
      to see.

'For, Lord, I was free of all Thy flowers, but I chose the
    world's sad roses,
    And that is why my feet are torn and mine eyes are blind
      with sweat,
But at Thy terrible judgment-seat, when this my tired life
    closes,
    I am ready to reap whereof I sowed, and pay my righteous
      debt.

'But once before the sand is run and the silver thread is
    broken,
    Give me a grace and cast aside the veil of dolorous
      years,
Grant me one hour of all mine hours, and let me see for a
    token
    Her pure and pitiful eyes shine out, and bathe her feet with
      tears.'

Her pitiful hands should calm, and her hair stream down and
    blind me,
    Out of the sight of night, and out of the reach of fear,

And her eyes should be my light whilst the sun went out
    behind me,
    And the viols in her voice be the last sound in mine ear.

Before the ruining waters fall and my life be carried under,
    And Thine anger cleave me through as a child cuts down a
    flower,
I will praise Thee, Lord, in Hell, while my limbs are racked
    asunder,
    For the last sad sight of her face and the little grace of an
    hour.

9

Fair is the world, now autumn's wearing,
And the sluggard sun lies long abed;
Sweet are the days, now winter's nearing,
And all winds feign that the wind is dead.

Dumb is the hedge where the crabs hang yellow,
Bright as the blossoms of the spring;
Dumb is the close where the pears grow mellow,
And none but the dauntless redbreasts sing.

Fair was the spring, but amidst his greening
Grey were the days of the hidden sun;
Fair was the summer, but overweening,
So soon his o'er-sweet days were done.

Come then, love, for peace is upon us,
Far off is failing, and far is fear,
Here where the rest in the end hath won us,
In the garnering tide of the happy year.

Come from the grey old house by the water,
Where, far from the lips of the hungry sea,
Green groweth the grass o'er the field of the slaughter,
And all is a tale for thee and me.

10

O golden love that waitest me,

The days pass on, pass on a-pace,
   Sometimes I have a little rest
In fairest dreams, when on thy face
   My lips lie, or thy hands are prest

About my forehead, and thy lips
   Draw near and nearer to mine own;
But when the vision from me slips,
   In colourless dawn I lie and moan,

And wander forth with fever'd blood,
   That makes me start at little things,
The blackbird screaming from the wood,
   The sudden whirr of pheasants' wings.

O dearest, scarcely seen by me—

II

Silence, loneliness, darkness—
   These, and of these my fill,
While God in the rush of the Maytide
   Without is working His will.

Without are the wind and the wall-flowers,
   The leaves and the nests and the rain;
And in all of them God is making
   His beautiful purpose plain.

But I wait in a horror of strangeness—
   A tool on His workshop floor,
Worn to the butt, and banished
   His hand for evermore.

12

My thoughts came drifting down the Prison where I lay
Through the Windows of their Wings the stars were
  shining—
The wings bore me away—the russet Wings and grey
With feathers like the moon-bleached Flowers—I was a God
  reclining:
Beneath me lay my Body's Chain and all the Dragons born
  of Pain
As I burned through the Prison Roof to walk on Pavement
  Shining.

The Wild Wind of Liberty swept through my Hair and sang
  beyond:
I heard the Souls of men asleep chattering in the Eaves
And rode on topmost Boughs of Heaven's single-moon-
  fruited Silver Wand,
Night's unifying Tree whereof the central Stars be leaves—
O Thoughts, Thoughts, Thoughts,—Fire-angel-birds relent-
  less—
Will you not brood in God's Star-tree and leave Red Heart
  tormentless!

13

O sähst du, voller Mondenschein,
Zum letztenmal auf meine Pein,
Den ich so manche Mitternacht
An diesem Pult herangewacht:
Dann, über Büchern und Papier,
Trübsel'ger Freund, erschienst du mir!
Ach! könnt' ich doch auf Berges-Höhn,
In deinem lieben Lichte gehn,
Um Bergeshöhle mit Geistern schweben,
Auf Wiesen in deinem Dämmer weben,
Von allem Wissensqualm entladen
In deinem Thau gesund mich baden!

14

Strange grows the river on the sunless evenings!
The river comforts me, grown spectral, vague and dumb:
Long was the day; at last the consoling shadows come:
Sufficient for the day are the day's evil things!

Labour and longing and despair the long day brings;
Patient till evening men watch the sun go west;
Deferred, expected night at last brings sleep and rest:
Sufficient for the day are the day's evil things!

At last the tranquil Angelus of evening rings
Night's curtain down for comfort and oblivion
Of all the vanities observèd by the sun:
Sufficient for the day are the day's evil things!

So, some time, when the last of all our evenings
Crowneth memorially the last of all our days,
Not loth to take his poppies man goes down and says,
'Sufficient for the day were the day's evil things!'

15

Who hath given man speech? or who hath set therein
A thorn for peril and a snare for sin?
For in the word his life is and his breath,
  And in the word his death,
That madness and the infatuate heart may breed
  From the word's womb the deed
And life bring one thing forth ere all pass by,
Even one thing which is ours yet cannot die—
Death. Hast thou seen him ever anywhere,
Time's twin-born brother, imperishable as he
Is perishable and plaintive, clothed with care
  And mutable as sand,
But death is strong and full of blood and fair
And perdurable and like a lord of land?
Nay, time thou seest not, death thou wilt not see
Till life's right hand be loosened from thine hand
  And thy life-days from thee.
For the gods very subtly fashion
  Madness with sadness upon earth:
Not knowing in any wise compassion,
  Nor holding pity of any worth;
And many things they have given and taken,
  And wrought and ruined many things;
The firm land have they loosed and shaken,
  And sealed the sea with all her springs;
They have wearied time with heavy burdens
  And vexed the lips of life with breath:
Set men to labour and given them guerdons,
  Death, and great darkness after death:

Put moans into the bridal measure
  And on the bridal wools a stain;
And circled pain about with pleasure,
  And girdled pleasure about with pain;
And strewed one marriage-bed with tears and fire
For extreme loathing and supreme desire.

What shall be done with all these tears of ours?
  Shall they make watersprings in the fair heaven
To bathe the brows of morning? or like flowers
Be shed and shine before the starriest hours,
  Or made the raiment of the weeping Seven?
Or rather, O our masters, shall they be
Food for the famine of the grievous sea,
  A great well-head of lamentation
Satiating the sad gods? or fall and flow
Among the years and seasons to and fro,
  And wash their feet with tribulation
And fill them full with grieving ere they go?

  Alas, our lords, and yet alas again,
Seeing all your iron heaven is gilt as gold
  But all we smite thereat in vain;
Smite the gates barred with groanings manifold,
  But all the floors are paven with our pain.
Yea, and with weariness of lips and eyes,
With breaking of the bosom, and with sighs,
  We labour, and are clad and fed with grief
And filled with days we would not fain behold
And nights we would not hear of; we wax old,
  All we wax old and wither like a leaf.
We are outcast, strayed between bright sun and moon;
  Our light and darkness are as leaves of flowers,

Black flowers and white, that perish; and the noon
　　As midnight, and the night as daylight hours.
　　A little fruit a little while is ours,
　　　　And the worm finds it soon.

But up in heaven the high gods one by one
　　Lay hands upon the draught that quickeneth,
Fulfilled with all tears shed and all things done,
　　And stir with soft imperishable breath
　　The bubbling bitterness of life and death,
And hold it to our lips and laugh; but they
Preserve their lips from tasting night or day,
　　Lest they too change and sleep, the fates that spun,
The lips that made us and the hands that slay;
　　Lest all these change, and heaven bow down to none,
Change and be subject to the secular sway
　　And terrene revolution of the sun.
Therefore they thrust it from them, putting time away.

I would the wine of time, made sharp and sweet
　　With multitudinous days and nights and tears
　　And many mixing savours of strange years,
Were no more trodden of them under feet,
　　Cast out and spilt about their holy places:
That life were given them as a fruit to eat
And death to drink as water; that the light
Might ebb, drawn backward from their eyes, and night
　　Hide for one hour the imperishable faces.
That they might rise up sad in heaven, and know
Sorrow and sleep, one paler than young snow,
　　One cold as blight of dew and ruinous rain;
Rise up and rest and suffer a little, and be
Awhile as all things born with us and we,
　　And grieve as men, and like slain men be slain.

88

For now we know not of them; but one saith
   The gods are gracious, praising God; and one,
When hast thou seen? or hast thou felt this breath
   Touch, nor consume thine eyelids as the sun,
Nor fill thee to the lips with fiery death?
   None hath beheld him, none
Seen above other gods and shapes of things,
Swift without feet and flying without wings,
Intolerable, not clad with death or life,
   Insatiable, not known of night or day,
The lord of love and loathing and of strife
   Who gives a star and takes a sun away;
Who shapes the soul, and makes her a barren wife
   To the earthly body and grievous growth of clay;
Who turns the large limbs to a little flame
   And binds the great sea with a little sand;
Who makes desire, and slays desire with shame;
   Who shakes the heaven as ashes in his hand;
Who, seeing the light and shadow for the same,
   Bids day waste night as fire devours a brand,
Smites without sword, and scourges without rod;
   The supreme evil, God.

Yea, with thine hate, O God, thou hast covered us,
   One saith, and hidden our eyes away from sight,
And made us transitory and hazardous,
   Light things and slight;
Yet have men praised thee, saying, He hath made man thus,
   And he doeth right.
Thou hast kissed us, and hast smitten; thou hast laid
Upon us with thy left hand life, and said,
Live: and again thou hast said, Yield up your breath,
And with thy right hand laid upon us death.
Thou hast sent us sleep, and stricken sleep with dreams,
   Saying, Joy is not, but love of joy shall be;

Thou hast made sweet springs for all the pleasant streams,
    In the end thou hast made them bitter with the sea.
Thou hast fed one rose with dust of many men;
    Thou hast marred one face with fire of many tears;
Thou hast taken love, and given us sorrow again;
    With pain thou hast filled us full to the eyes and ears.
Therefore because thou art strong, our father, and we
    Feeble; and thou art against us, and thine hand
Constrains us in the shallows of the sea
    And breaks us at the limits of the land;
Because thou hast bent thy lightnings as a bow,
    And loosed the hours like arrows; and let fall
Sins and wild words and many a wingèd woe
    And wars among us, and one end of all;
Because thou hast made the thunder, and thy feet
    Are as a rushing water when the skies
Break, but thy face as an exceeding heat
    And flames of fire the eyelids of thine eyes;
Because thou art over all who are over us;
    Because thy name is life and our name death;
Because thou art cruel and men are piteous,
    And our hands labour and thine hand scattereth;
Lo, with hearts rent and knees made tremulous,
    Lo, with ephemeral lips and casual breath,
      At least we witness of thee ere we die
That these things are not otherwise, but thus;
    That each man in his heart sigheth, and saith,
      That all men even as I,
All we are against thee, against thee, O God most high.

None hath beheld him, none
Seen above other gods and shapes of things
Swift without feet and flying without wings
Intolerable, not clad with death or life,
Insatiable, not known of night or day,
The lord of love and loathing and of strife
Who gives a star and takes a sun away:
Who shapes the soul, and makes her a barren wife
To the earthly body and grievous growth of clay:
Who turns the large limbs to a little flame
And binds the great sea with a little sand:
Who makes desire, and slays desire with shame
Who shakes the heaven as ashes in his hand
Who, seeing the light and shadow for the same
Bids day waste night as fire devours a brand,
Smites without sword, and scourges without rod
The supreme evil, God.

Yea, with thine hate, O God, thou hast covered us
One saith, and hidden our eyes away from sight,
And made us transitory and hazardous
Light things, and slight,
Yet have men praised thee, saying He hath made man thus
And he doeth right.

Thou hast kissed us, and hast smitten: thou hast laid
Upon us with thy left hand life, and said
Live: and again thou hast said, Yield up your breath
And with thy right hand laid upon us death.
Thou hast sent us sleep, and stricken sleep with dreams
Saying Joy is not, but love of joy shall be:
Thou hast made sweet springs for all the pleasant streams
In the end thou hast made them bitter with the sea.
Thou hast fed one rose with dust of many men
Thou hast marred one face with fire of many tears.
Thou hast taken love and given us sorrow again
With pain thou hast filled us full to the eyes and ears.
Therefore because thou art strong, our father, and we
Feeble: and thou art against us, and thine hand
Constrains us in the shallows of the sea
And breaks us at the limits of the land:
Because thou hast bent thy lightnings as a bow
And loosed the hours like arrows: and let fall
Sins and wild words and many a winged woe
And wars among us, and one end of all:
Because thou hast made the thunder, and thy feet
Are as a rushing water when the skies
Break, but thy face as an exceeding heat
And flames of fire the eyelids of thine eyes:
Because thou art over all who are over us
Because thy name is life and our name death
Because thou art cruel and men are piteous,
And our hands labour and thine hand scattereth
Lo with hearts rent, and knees made tremulous
Lo with ephemeral lips and casual breath
At least we witness of thee ere we die
That these things are not otherwise, but thus.
That each man in his heart sigheth and saith
That all men even as I
All we are against thee, against thee, O God most high.

16

Not unto us, O Lord,
Not unto us the rapture of the day,
The peace of night, or love's divine surprise,
High heart, high speech, high deeds 'mid honouring eyes;
For at Thy word
All these are taken away.

Not unto us, O Lord:
To us thou givest the scorn, the scourge, the scar,
The ache of life, the loneliness of death,
The insufferable sufficiency of breath;
And with Thy sword
Thou piercest very far.

Not unto us, O Lord:
Nay, Lord, but unto her be all things given—
May light and life and earth and sky be blasted—
But let not all that wealth of love be wasted:
Let Hell afford
The pavement of her Heaven!

17

Wilt Thou forgive that sin where I begun,
  Which was my sin, though it were done before?
Wilt Thou forgive that sin through which I run,
  And do run still, though still I do deplore?
When Thou hast done, Thou hast not done;
    For I have more.

Wilt Thou forgive that sin which I have won
  Others to sin, and made my sins their door?
Wilt Thou forgive that sin which I did shun
  A year or two, but wallow'd in a score?
When Thou hast done, Thou hast not done;
    For I have more.

I have a sin of fear, that when I've spun
  My last thread, I shall perish on the shore;
But swear by Thyself that at my death Thy Son
  Shall shine as He shines now and heretofore:
And having done that, Thou hast done;
    I fear no more.

18

'O what can ail thee, knight-at-arms,
    Alone and palely loitering?
The sedge is wither'd from the lake,
    And no birds sing.

O what can ail thee, knight-at-arms,
    So haggard and so woe-begone?
The squirrel's granary is full,
    And the harvest's done.

'I see a lily on thy brow
    With anguish moist and fever dew;
And on thy cheek a fading rose
    Fast withereth too.'

'I met a lady in the meads,
    Full beautiful—a faery's child,
Her hair was long, her foot was light,
    And her eyes were wild.

'I made a garland for her head,
    And bracelets too, and fragrant zone;
She look'd at me as she did love,
    And made sweet moan.

'I set her on my pacing steed
    And nothing else saw all day long,
For sideways would she lean, and sing
    A faery's song.

'She found me roots of relish sweet,
    And honey wild and manna dew,
And sure in language strange she said,
    "I love thee true!"

'She took me to her elfin grot,
    And there she wept and sigh'd full sore;
And there I shut her wild, wild eyes
    With kisses four.

'And there she lullèd me asleep,
    And there I dream'd—Ah! woe betide!
The latest dream I ever dream'd
    On the cold hill's side.

'I saw pale kings and princes too,
    Pale warriors, death-pale were they all;
Who cried—"La belle Dame sans Merci
    Hath thee in thrall!"

'I saw their starved lips in the gloam
    With horrid warning gapèd wide,
And I awoke and found me here
    On the cold hill's side.

'And this is why I sojourn here
    Alone and palely loitering,
Though the sedge is wither'd from the lake,
    And no birds sing.'

19

My new-cut ashlar takes the light
  Where crimson-blank the windows flare;
By my own work, before the night,
  Great Overseer, I make my prayer.

If there be good in that I wrought,
  Thy hand compell'd it, Master, Thine;
Where I have fail'd to meet Thy thought
  I know, through Thee, the blame is mine.

One instant's toil to Thee denied
  Stands all Eternity's offence;
Of that I did with Thee to guide
  To Thee, through Thee, be excellence.

Who, lest all thought of Eden fade,
  Bring'st Eden to the craftsman's brain,
Godlike to muse o'er his own trade
  And manlike stand with God again.

The depth and dream of my desire,
  The bitter paths wherein I stray,
Thou knowest Who hast made the Fire,
  Thou knowest Who hast made the Clay.

One stone the more swings to her place
  In that dread Temple of Thy worth—
It is enough that through Thy grace
  I saw naught common on Thy earth.

Take not that vision from my ken;
　O, whatsoe'er may spoil or speed,
Help me to need no aid from men,
　That I may help such men as need!

20

Helen, thy beauty is to me
  Like those Nicèan barks of yore
That gently, o'er a perfumed sea,
  The weary way-worn wanderer bore
  To his own native shore.

On desperate seas long wont to roam,
  Thy hyacinth hair, thy classic face,
Thy Naiad airs have brought me home
  To the glory that was Greece,
And the grandeur that was Rome.

Lo, in yon brilliant window-niche
  How statue-like I see thee stand,
  The agate lamp within thy hand,
Ah! Psyche, from the regions which
  Are holy land!

21

They told me, Heraclitus, they told me you were dead,
They brought me bitter news to hear and bitter tears to shed.
I wept as I remember'd how often you and I
Had tired the sun with talking and sent him down the sky.

And now that thou art lying, my dear old Carian guest,
A handful of grey ashes, long, long ago at rest,
Still are thy pleasant voices, thy nightingales, awake;
For Death, he taketh all away, but them he cannot take.

22

This ae nighte, this ae nighte,
  —*Every nighte and alle,*
Fire and sleet and candle-lighte,
  And Christe receive thy saule.

When thou from hence away art past,
  —*Every nighte and alle,*
To Whinny-muir thou com'st at last;
  And Christe receive thy saule.

If ever thou gavest hosen and shoon,
  —*Every nighte and alle,*
Sit thee down and put them on;
  And Christe receive thy saule.

If hosen and shoon thou ne'er gav'st nane,
  —*Every nighte and alle,*
The whinnes sall prick thee to the bare bane;
  And Christe receive thy saule.

From Whinny-muir when thou may'st pass,
  —*Every nighte and alle,*
To Brig o' Dread thou com'st at last;
  And Christe receive thy saule.

From Brig o' Dread when thou may'st pass,
  —*Every nighte and alle,*
To Purgatory fire thou com'st at last;
  And Christe receive thy saule.

If ever thou gavest meat or drink,
    — Every nighte and alle,
The fire sall never make thee shrink;
    And Christe receive thy saule.

If meat or drink thou ne'er gav'st nane,
    — Every nighte and alle,
The fire will burn thee to the bare bane;
    And Christe receive thy saule.

This ae nighte, this ae nighte,
    — Every nighte and alle,
Fire and sleet and candle-lighte,
    And Christe receive thy saule.

23

Come live with me and be my Love,
And we will all the pleasures prove
That hills and valleys, dales and fields,
Or woods or steepy mountain yields.

And we will sit upon the rocks,
And see the shepherds feed their flocks
By shallow rivers, to whose falls
Melodious birds sing madrigals.

And I will make thee beds of roses
And a thousand fragrant posies;
A cap of flowers, and a kirtle
Embroider'd all with leaves of myrtle.

A gown made of the finest wool
Which from our pretty lambs we pull;
Fair-linèd slippers for the cold,
With buckles of the purest gold.

A belt of straw and ivy-buds
With coral clasps and amber studs:
And if these pleasures may thee move,
Come live with me and be my Love.

The shepherd swains shall dance and sing
For thy delight each May morning:
If these delights thy mind may move,
Then live with me and be my Love.

24

Yes: in the sea of life enisled,
 With echoing straits between us thrown,
Dotting the shoreless watery wild,
 We mortal millions live *alone*.
The islands feel the enclasping flow,
And then their endless bounds they know.

But when the moon their hollows lights,
 And they are swept by balms of spring,
And in their glens, on starry nights,
 The nightingales divinely sing;
And lovely notes, from shore to shore,
Across the sounds and channels pour;

O then a longing like despair
 Is to their farthest caverns sent!
For surely once, they feel, we were
 Parts of a single continent.
Now round us spreads the watery plain—
O might our marges meet again!

Who order'd that their longing's fire
 Should be, as soon as kindled, cool'd?
Who renders vain their deep desire?—
 A God, a God their severance ruled;
And bade betwixt their shores to be
The unplumb'd, salt, estranging sea.

25

When God at first made Man,
Having a glass of blessings standing by—
Let us (said He) pour on him all we can;
Let the world's riches, which dispersèd lie,
    Contract into a span.

So strength first made a way,
Then beauty flow'd, then wisdom, honour, pleasure:
When almost all was out, God made a stay,
Perceiving that, alone of all His treasure,
    Rest in the bottom lay.

For if I should (said He)
Bestow this jewel also on My creature,
He would adore My gifts instead of Me,
And rest in Nature, not the God of Nature:
    So both should losers be.

Yet let him keep the rest,
But keep them with repining restlessness;
Let him be rich and weary, that at least,
If goodness lead him not, yet weariness
    May toss him to My breast.

26

Pray but one prayer for me 'twixt thy closed lips,
Think but one thought of me up in the stars.
   The summer night waneth, the morning light slips,
Faint & grey 'twixt the leaves of the aspen, betwixt the
      cloud-bars,
That are patiently waiting there for the dawn:
   Patient and colourless, though Heaven's gold
Waits to float through them along with the sun.
Far out in the meadows, above the young corn,
   The heavy elms wait, and restless and cold
The uneasy wind rises; the roses are dun;
Through the long twilight they pray for the dawn.
Round the lone house in the midst of the corn.
   Speak but one word to me over the corn,
   Over the tender, bow'd locks of the corn.

27

Wearily, drearily,
Half the day long,
Flap the great banners
High over the stone;
Strangely and eerily
Sounds the wind's song,
Bending the banner-poles.

While, all alone,
Watching the loophole's spark,
Lie I, with life all dark,
Feet tether'd, hands fetter'd
Fast to the stone,
The grim walls, square-letter'd
With prison'd men's groan.

Still strain the banner-poles
Through the wind's song,
Westward the banner rolls
Over my wrong.

28

So fair, so sweet, withal so sensitive,
Would that the little Flowers were born to live,
Conscious of half the pleasure which they give;

That to this mountain-daisy's self were known
The beauty of its star-shaped shadow, thrown
On the smooth surface of this naked stone!

And what if hence a bold desire should mount
High as the Sun, that he could take account
Of all that issues from his glorious fount!

So might he ken how by his sovereign aid
These delicate companionships are made;
And how he rules the pomp of light and shade;

And were the Sister-power that shines by night
So privileged, what a countenance of delight
Would through the clouds break forth on human sight!

29

Downhill I came, hungry, and yet not starved;
Cold, yet had heat within me that was proof
Against the North wind; tired, yet so that rest
Had seemed the sweetest thing under a roof.

Then at the inn I had food, fire, and rest,
Knowing how hungry, cold, and tired was I.
All of the night was quite barred out except
An owl's cry, a most melancholy cry

Shaken out long and clear upon the hill,
No merry note, nor cause of merriment,
But one telling me plain what I escaped
And others could not, that night, as in I went.

And salted was my food, and my repose,
Salted and sobered, too, by the bird's voice
Speaking for all who lay under the stars,
Soldiers and poor, unable to rejoice.

30

In the hour of death, after this life's whim,
When the heart beats low, and the eyes grow dim,
And pain has exhausted every limb—
    The lover of the Lord shall trust in Him.

When the will has forgotten the lifelong aim,
And the mind can only disgrace its fame,
And a man is uncertain of his own name—
    The power of the Lord shall fill this frame.

When the last sigh is heaved, and the last tear shed,
And the coffin is waiting beside the bed,
And the widow and child forsake the dead—
    The angel of the Lord shall lift this head.

For even the purest delight may pall,
And power must fail, and the pride must fall,
And the love of the dearest friends grow small—
    But the glory of the Lord is all in all.

31

Our birth is but a sleep and a forgetting:
The Soul that rises with us, our life's Star,
   Hath had elsewhere its setting,
     And cometh from afar:
   Not in entire forgetfulness,
   And not in utter nakedness,
But trailing clouds of glory do we come
   From God, who is our home:
Heaven lies about us in our infancy!

Shades of the prison-house begin to close
   Upon the growing Boy,
But he beholds the light, and whence it flows,
   He sees it in his joy;
The Youth, who daily farther from the east
   Must travel, still is Nature's priest,
     And by the vision splendid
     Is on his way attended;
At length the Man perceives it die away,
And fade into the light of common day.

32

To live within a cave—it is most good;
  But, if God make a day,
  And some one come, and say,
'Lo! I have gather'd faggots in the wood!'
  E'en let him stay,
And light a fire, and fan a temporal mood!

So sit till morning! when the light is grown
  That he the path can read,
  Then bid the man God-speed!
His morning is not thine: yet must thou own.
They have a cheerful warmth—those ashes on the stone.

33

You meaner beauties of the night,
   That poorly satisfy our eyes
More by your number than your light,
   You common people of the skies;
   What are you when the moon shall rise?

You curious chanters of the wood,
   That warble forth Dame Nature's lays,
Thinking your passions understood
   By your weak accents; what's your praise
   When Philomel her voice shall raise?

You violets that first appear,
   By your pure purple mantles known
Like the proud virgins of the year,
   As if the spring were all your own;
   What are you when the rose is blown?

34

Love bade me welcome; yet my soul drew back,
   Guilty of dust and sin.
But quick-eyed Love, observing me grow slack
   From my first entrance in,
Drew nearer to me, sweetly questioning
   If I lack'd anything.

'A guest,' I answer'd, 'worthy to be here:'
   Love said, 'You shall be he.'
'I, the unkind, ungrateful? Ah, my dear,
   I cannot look on Thee.'
Love took my hand and smiling did reply,
   'Who made the eyes but I?'

'Truth, Lord; but I have marr'd them: let my shame
   Go where it doth deserve.'
'And know you not,' says Love, 'Who bore the blame?'
   'My dear, then I will serve.'
'You must sit down,' says Love, 'and taste my meat.'
   So I did sit and eat.

35

'Not ours,' say some, 'the thought of death to dread;
　　Asking no heaven, we fear no fabled hell:
Life is a feast, and we have banqueted—
　　Shall not the worms as well?

'The after-silence, when the feast is o'er,
　　And void the places where the minstrels stood,
Differs in nought from what hath been before,
　　And is nor ill nor good.'

Ah, but the Apparition—the dumb sign—
　　The beckoning finger bidding me forgo
The fellowship, the converse, and the wine,
　　The songs, the festal glow!

And ah, to know not, while with friends I sit,
　　And while the purple joy is pass'd about,
Whether 'tis ampler day divinelier lit
　　Or homeless night without;

And whether, stepping forth, my soul shall see
　　New prospects, or fall sheer—a blinded thing!
There is, O grave, thy hourly victory,
　　And there, O death, thy sting.

36

Verse, a breeze 'mid blossoms straying,
Where Hope clung feeding, like a bee—
Both were mine! Life went a-maying
With Nature, Hope, and Poesy,
    When I was young!

Flowers are lovely! Love is flower-like;
Friendship is a sheltering tree;
O the joys, that came down shower-like,
Of Friendship, Love, and Liberty,
    Ere I was old!

Dewdrops are the gems of morning,
But the tears of mournful eve!
Where no hope is, life's a warning
That only serves to make us grieve,
    When we are old!

That only serves to make us grieve
With oft and tedious taking-leave,
Like some poor nigh-related guest
That may not rudely be dismist.
Yet hath outstay'd his welcome while,
And tells the jest without the smile.

37

The glories of our blood and state
　　Are shadows, not substantial things;
There is no armour against Fate;
　　Death lays his icy hand on kings:
　　　　Sceptre and Crown
　　　　Must tumble down,
And in the dust be equal made
With the poor crookèd scythe and spade.

Some men with swords may reap the field,
　　And plant fresh laurels where they kill:
But their strong nerves at last must yield;
　　They tame but one another still:
　　　　Early or late
　　　　They stoop to fate,
And must give up their murmuring breath
When they, pale captives, creep to death.

The garlands wither on your brow;
　　Then boast no more your mighty deeds!
Upon Death's purple altar now
　　See where the victor-victim bleeds.
　　　　Your heads must come
　　　　To the cold tomb:
Only the actions of the just
Smell sweet and blossom in their dust.

38

The wine of Love is music,
   And the feast of Love is song:
And when Love sits down to the banquet,
   Love sits long:

Sits long and ariseth drunken,
   But not with the feast and the wine;
He reeleth with his own heart,
   That great rich Vine.

39

My love is the flaming Sword
  To fight through the world;
Thy love is the Shield to ward,
And the Armour of the Lord
  And the Banner of Heaven unfurled.

40

Too late for love, too late for joy,
   Too late, too late!
You loiter'd on the road too long,
   You trifled at the gate:
The enchanted dove upon her branch
   Died without a mate;
The enchanted princess in her tower
   Slept, died, behind the grate;
Her heart was starving all this while
   You made it wait.

Ten years ago, five years ago,
   One year ago,
Even then you had arrived in time,
   Though somewhat slow;
Then you had known her living face
   Which now you cannot know:
The frozen fountain would have leap'd,
   The buds gone on to blow,
The warm south wind would have awaked
   To melt the snow.

You should have wept her yesterday,
   Wasting upon her bed:
But wherefore should you weep to-day
   That she is dead?
Lo, we who love weep not to-day,
   But crown her royal head.

Let be these poppies that we strew,
  Your roses are too red:
Let be these poppies, not for you
  Cut down and spread.

41

In Xanadu did Kubla Khan
   A stately pleasure-dome decree:
Where Alph, the sacred river, ran
Through caverns measureless to man
   Down to a sunless sea.
So twice five miles of fertile ground
   With walls and towers were girdled round:
And there were gardens bright with sinuous rills
Where blossom'd many an incense-bearing tree;
And here were forests ancient as the hills,
Enfolding sunny spots of greenery.

But O, that deep romantic chasm which slanted
Down the green hill athwart a cedarn cover!
A savage place! as holy and enchanted
As e'er beneath a waning moon was haunted
By woman wailing for her demon-lover!
And from this chasm, with ceaseless turmoil seething,
As if this earth in fast thick pants were breathing,
A mighty fountain momently was forced;
Amid whose swift half-intermitted burst
Huge fragments vaulted like rebounding hail,
Or chaffy grain beneath the thresher's flail:
And 'mid these dancing rocks at once and ever
It flung up momently the sacred river.
Five miles meandering with a mazy motion
Through wood and dale the sacred river ran,
Then reach'd the caverns measureless to man,
And sank in tumult to a lifeless ocean:

And 'mid this tumult Kubla heard from far
Ancestral voices prophesying war!

The shadow of the dome of pleasure
    Floated midway on the waves;
Where was heard the mingled measure
    From the fountain and the caves.
It was a miracle of rare device,
A sunny pleasure-dome with caves of ice!

A damsel with a dulcimer
    In a vision once I saw:
It was an Abyssinian maid,
    And on her dulcimer she play'd,
Singing of Mount Abora.
Could I revive within me,
    Her symphony and song,
To such a deep delight 'twould win me,
That with music loud and long,
I would build that dome in air,
That sunny dome! those caves of ice!
And all who heard should see them there,
And all should cry, Beware! Beware!
His flashing eyes, his floating hair!
Weave a circle round him thrice,
    And close your eyes with holy dread,
    For he on honey-dew hath fed,
And drunk the milk of Paradise.

In Xanadu did Kubla Khan
A stately pleasure - dome decree
Where Alph the sacred river ran
Through caverns measureless to man
Down to a sunless sea
So twice five miles of fertile ground
With walls and towers were girdled round:
And there were gardens bright with sinuous rills
Where blossomed many an incense - bearing tree;
And here were forests ancient as the hills
Enfolding sunny spots of greenery.

But O, that deep romantic chasm which slanted
Down the green hill athwart a cedarn cover!
A savage place! as holy and enchanted
As e'er beneath a waning moon was haunted
By woman wailing for her demon - lover!
And from this chasm, with ceaseless turmoil seething
As if this earth in fast thick pants were breathing
A mighty fountain momently was forced:
Amid whose swift half - intermitted burst
Huge fragments vaulted like rebounding hail
Or chaffy grain beneath the thresher's flail:
And mid these dancing rocks at once and ever
It flung up momently the sacred river.
Five miles meandering with a mazy motion
Through wood and dale the sacred river ran
Then reached the caverns measureless to man
And sank in tumult to a lifeless ocean:
And mid this tumult Kubla heard from far
Ancestral voices prophesying war!
The shadow of the dome of pleasure
Floated midway on the waves:
Where was heard the mingled measure
From the fountain and the caves.
        It was a miracle of rare device
        A sunny pleasure - dome with caves of ice!
A damsel with a dulcimer
In a vision once I saw:
It was an Abyssinian maid
And on her dulcimer she played
Singing of Mount Abora.
Could I revive within me
Her symphony and song
To such a deep delight 'twould win me
That with music loud and long
I would build that dome in air,
That sunny dome! those caves of ice!
And all who heard should see them there
And all should cry Beware! Beware!
His flashing eyes, his floating hair!
Weave a circle round him thrice
And close your eyes with holy dread
        For he on honey - dew hath fed
        And drunk the milk of Paradise.

42

Everyone suddenly burst out singing;
And I was filled with such delight
As prisoned birds must find in freedom,
Winging wildly across the white
Orchards and dark-green fields; on—on—and out of sight.

Everyone's voice was suddenly lifted;
And beauty came like the setting sun:
My heart was shaken with tears; and horror
Drifted away ... O, but Everyone
Was a bird; and the song was wordless; the singing will
    never be done.

43

My heart aches, and a drowsy numbness pains
   My sense, as though of hemlock I had drunk,
Or emptied some dull opiate to the drains
   One minute past, and Lethe-wards had sunk:
'Tis not through envy of thy happy lot,
   But being too happy in thy happiness,
      That thou, light-wingèd Dryad of the trees,
        In some melodious plot
   Of beechen green, and shadows numberless,
      Singest of summer in full-throated ease.

O for a draught of vintage! that hath been
   Cool'd a long age in the deep-delvèd earth,
Tasting of Flora and the country-green,
   Dance, and Provençal song, and sunburnt mirth!
O for a beaker full of the warm South!
   Full of the true, the blushful Hippocrene,
      With beaded bubbles winking at the brim,
        And purple-stainèd mouth;
That I might drink, and leave the world unseen,
   And with thee fade away into the forest dim:

Fade far away, dissolve, and quite forget
   What thou among the leaves hast never known,
The weariness, the fever, and the fret
   Here, where men sit and hear each other groan;
Where palsy shakes a few, sad, last grey hairs,
   Where youth grows pale, and spectre-thin, and dies;
      Where but to think is to be full of sorrow
        And leaden-eyed despairs;

Where beauty cannot keep her lustrous eyes,
    Or new Love pine at them beyond to-morrow.

Away! away! for I will fly to thee,
    Not charioted by Bacchus and his pards,
But on the viewless wings of Poesy,
    Though the dull brain perplexes and retards:
Already with thee! tender is the night,
    And haply the Queen-Moon is on her throne,
        Cluster'd around by all her starry Fays;
            But here there is no light,
    Save what from heaven is with the breezes blown
        Through verdurous glooms and winding mossy ways.

I cannot see what flowers are at my feet,
    Nor what soft incense hangs upon the boughs,
But, in embalmèd darkness, guess each sweet
    Wherewith the seasonable month endows
The grass, the thicket, and the fruit-tree wild;
    White hawthorn, and the pastoral eglantine;
        Fast-fading violets cover'd up in leaves;
            And mid-May's eldest child,
    The coming musk-rose, full of dewy wine,
        The murmurous haunt of flies on summer eves.

Darkling I listen; and for many a time
    I have been half in love with easeful Death,
Call'd him soft names in many a musèd rhyme,
    To take into the air my quiet breath;
Now more than ever seems it rich to die,
    To cease upon the midnight with no pain,
        While thou art pouring forth thy soul abroad
            In such an ecstasy!
    Still wouldst thou sing, and I have ears in vain—
        To thy high requiem become a sod.

Thou wast not born for death, immortal Bird!
  No hungry generations tread thee down;
The voice I hear this passing night was heard
  In ancient days by emperor and clown:
Perhaps the self-same song that found a path
    Through the sad heart of Ruth, when, sick for home,
      She stood in tears amid the alien corn;
        The same that ofttimes hath
    Charm'd magic casements, opening on the foam
    Of perilous seas, in faery lands forlorn.

Forlorn! the very word is like a bell
  To toll me back from thee to my sole self!
Adieu! the fancy cannot cheat so well
  As she is famed to do, deceiving elf.
Adieu! adieu! thy plaintive anthem fades
    Past the near meadows, over the still stream,
      Up the hill-side; and now 'tis buried deep
        In the next valley-glades:
    Was it a vision, or a waking dream?
    Fled is that music:—do I wake or sleep?

44

If you could crowd them into forty lines!
Yes; you can do it, once you get a start;
All that you want is waiting in your head,
For long-ago you've learnt it off by heart.

.   .   .   .   .

Begin: your mind's the room where you have slept,
(Don't pause for rhymes), till twilight woke you early.
The window stands wide-open, as it stood
When tree-tops loomed enchanted for a child
Hearing the dawn's first thrushes through the wood
Warbling (you know the words) serene and wild.

You've said it all before: you dreamed of Death,
A dim Apollo in the bird-voiced breeze
That drifts across the morning veiled with showers,
While golden weather shines among dark trees.

You've got your limitations; let them sing,
And all your life will waken with a cry:
Why should you halt when rapture's on the wing
And you've no limit but the cloud-flocked sky? ...

But some chap shouts, 'Here, stop it; that's been done!'—
As God might holloa to the rising sun,
And then relent, because the glorying rays
Remind Him of green-glinting Eden days,
And Adam's trustful eyes as he looks up
From carving eagles on his beechwood cup.

Young Adam knew his job; he could condense
Life to an eagle from the unknown immense ...
Go on, whoever you are; your lines can be
A whisper in the music from the weirs
Of song that plunge and tumble toward the sea
That is the uncharted mercy of our tears.

.   .   .   .   .

I told you it was easy! ... Words are fools
Who follow blindly, once they get a lead.
But thoughts are kingfishers that haunt the pools
Of quiet; seldom-seen: and all you need
Is just that flash of joy above your dream.
So, when those forty platitudes are done,
You'll hear a bird-note calling from the stream
That wandered through your childhood; and the sun
Will strike the old flaming wonder from the waters ...
And there'll be forty lines not yet begun.

45

Eve, with her basket, was
Deep in the bells and grass,
Wading in bells and grass
Up to her knees,
Picking a dish of sweet
Berries and plums to eat,
Down in the bells and grass
Under the trees.

Mute as a mouse in a
Corner the cobra lay,
Curled round a bough of the
Cinnamon tall ...
Now to get even and
Humble proud heaven and
Now was the moment or
Never at all.

'Eva!' Each syllable
Light as a flower fell,
'Eva!' he whispered the
Wondering maid,
Soft as a bubble sung
Out of a linnet's lung,
Soft and most silverly
'Eva!' he said.

Picture that orchard sprite,
Eve, with her body white,
Supple and smooth to her
Slim finger tips,

Wondering, listening,
Listening, wondering,
Eve with a berry
Half-way to her lips.

Oh had our simple Eve
Seen through the make-believe!
Had she but known the
Pretender he was!
Out of the boughs he came,
Whispering still her name,
Tumbling in twenty rings
Into the grass.

Here was the strangest pair
In the world anywhere,
Eve in the bells and grass
Kneeling, and he
Telling his story low ...
Singing birds saw them go
Down the dark path to
The Blasphemous Tree.

Oh what a clatter when
Titmouse and Jenny Wren
Saw him successful and
Taking his leave!
How the birds rated him,
How they all hated him!
How they all pitied
Poor motherless Eve!

Picture her crying
Outside in the lane,
Eve, with no dish of sweet

Berries and plums to eat,
Haunting the gate of the
Orchard in vain ...
Picture the lewd delight
Under the hill to-night—
'Eva!' the toast goes round,
'Eva!' again.

46

When I was young my heart and head were light,
And I was gay and feckless as a colt
Out in the fields, with morning in the may,
Wind on the grass, wings in the orchard bloom.
  O thrilling sweet, my joy, when life was free,
  And all the paths led on from hawthorn-time
  Across the carolling meadows into June.

But now my heart is heavy-laden. I sit
Burning my dreams away beside the fire:
For death has made me wise and bitter and strong;
And I am rich in all that I have lost.
  O starshine on the fields of long-ago,
  Bring me the darkness and the nightingale;
  Dim wealds of vanished summer, peace of home,
  And silence; and the faces of my friends.

47

Why do you lie with your legs ungainly huddled,
And one arm bent across your sullen, cold,
Exhausted face? It hurts my heart to watch you,
Deep-shadow'd from the candle's guttering gold;
And you wonder why I shake you by the shoulder;
Drowsy, you mumble and sigh and turn your head ...
You are too young to fall asleep for ever;
And when you sleep you remind me of the dead.

Why do you lie with your legs ungainly huddled,
And one arm bent across your sullen cold
Exhausted face? It hurts my heart to watch you,
Deep-shadowed from the candle's guttering gold:
And you wonder why I shake you by the shoulder;
Drowsy, you mumble and sigh and turn your head .....
You are too young to fall asleep for ever;
And when you sleep you remind me of the dead.

48

To-night this sunset spreads two golden wings
    Cleaving the western sky;
Winged too with wind it is, and winnowings
Of birds; as if the day's last hour in rings
    Of strenuous flight must die.

Sun-steeped in fire, the homeward pinions sway
    Above the dovecote-tops;
And clouds of starlings, ere they rest with day,
Sink, clamorous like mill-waters, at wild play,
    By turns in every copse:

Each tree heart-deep the wrangling rout receives,—
    Save for the whirr within,
You could not tell the starlings from the leaves;
Then one great puff of wings, and the swarm heaves
    Away with all its din.

Even thus Hope's hours, in ever-eddying flight,
    To many a refuge tend;
With the first light she laughed, and the last light
Glows round her still; who natheless in the night
    At length must make an end.

And now the mustering rooks innumerable
    Together sail and soar,
While for the day's death, like a tolling knell,
Unto the heart they seem to cry, Farewell,
    No more, farewell, no more!

Is Hope not plumed, as 'twere a fiery dart?
   And oh! thou dying day,
Even as thou goest must she too depart,
And Sorrow fold such pinions on the heart
   As will not fly away?

49

He came and took me by the hand
   Up to a red rose tree,
He kept His meaning to Himself
   But gave a rose to me.

I did not pray Him to lay bare
   The mystery to me,
Enough the rose was Heaven to smell,
   And His own face to see.

50

If there were dreams to sell,
   What would you buy?
Some cost a passing bell;
   Some a light sigh,
That shakes from Life's fresh crown
Only a rose-leaf down.
If there were dreams to sell,
Merry and sad to tell,
And the crier rang the bell,
   What would you buy?

A cottage lone and still,
   With bowers nigh,
Shadowy, my wants to still,
   Until they die.
Such peace from Life's fresh crown
Fain would I shake me down.
Were dreams to have at will,
This would best heal my ill,
   This would I buy.

51

Yet if His Majesty, our sovereign lord,
Should of his own accord
Friendly himself invite,
And say 'I'll be your guest to-morrow night,'
How should we stir ourselves, call and command
All hands to work! 'Let no man idle stand!

'Set me fine Spanish tables in the hall;
See they be fitted all;
Let there be room to eat
And order taken that there want no meat.
See every sconce and candlestick made bright,
That without tapers they may give a light.

'Look to the presence: are the carpets spread,
The dazie o'er the head,
The cushions in the chairs,
And all the candles lighted on the stairs?
Perfume the chambers, and in any case
Let each man give attendance in his place!'

Thus, if a king were coming, would we do;
And 'twere good reason too;
For 'tis a duteous thing
To show all honour to an earthly king,
And after all our travail and our cost,
So he be pleased, to think no labour lost.

But at the coming of the King of Heaven
All's set at six and seven;
We wallow in our sin,
Christ cannot find a chamber in the inn.
We entertain Him always like a stranger,
And, as at first, still lodge Him in the manger.

52

Say not the struggle naught availeth,
  The labour and the wounds are vain,
The enemy faints not, nor faileth,
  And as things have been they remain.

If hopes were dupes, fears may be liars;
  It may be, in yon smoke conceal'd,
Your comrades chase e'en now the fliers,
  And, but for you, possess the field.

For while the tired waves, vainly breaking,
  Seem here no painful inch to gain,
Far back, through creeks and inlets making,
  Comes silent, flooding in, the main.

And not by eastern windows only,
  When daylight comes, comes in the light;
In front the sun climbs slow, how slowly!
  But westward, look, the land is bright!

53

Let my voice ring out and over the earth,
  Through all the grief and strife,
With a golden joy in a silver mirth:
  Thank God for Life!

Let my voice swell out through the great abyss.
  To the azure dome above,
With a chord of faith in the harp of bliss:
  Thank God for Love!

Let my voice thrill out beneath and above,
  The whole world through:
O my Love and Life, O my Life and Love,
  Thank God for you!

54

The day is dark and the night
   To him that would search their heart;
   No lips of cloud that will part
Nor morning song in the light:
   Only, gazing alone,
   To him wild shadows are shown,
   Deep under deep unknown
And height above unknown height.
        Still we say as we go,—
          'Strange to think by the way,
        Whatever there is to know,
          That shall we know one day.'

The Past is over and fled;
   Named new, we name it the old;
   Thereof some tale hath been told,
But no word comes from the dead;
   Whether at all they be,
   Or whether as bond or free,
   Or whether they too were we,
Or by what spell they have sped.
        Still we say as we go,—
          'Strange to think by the way,
        Whatever there is to know,
          That shall we know one day.'

What of the heart of hate
   That beats in thy breast, O Time?—
   Red strife from the furthest prime,

And anguish of fierce debate
   War that shatters her slain,
   And peace that grinds them as grain,
   And eyes fixed ever in vain
On the pitiless eyes of Fate.
      Still we say as we go,—
        'Strange to think by the way,
     Whatever there is to know,
       That shall we know one day.'

The sky leans dumb on the sea,
   Aweary with all its wings;
   And oh! the song the sea sings
Is dark everlastingly.
   Our past is clean forgot,
   Our present is and is not,
   Our future's a sealed seedplot,
And what betwixt them are we?—
      We who say as we go,—
        'Strange to think by the way,
     Whatever there is to know,
       That shall we know one day.'

55

I looked out into the morning,
  I looked out into the west:
The soft blue eye of the quiet sky
  Still drooped in dreamy rest;

The trees were still like clouds there
  The clouds like mountains dim;
The broad mist lay, a silver bay
  Whose tide was at the brim.

I looked out into the morning,
  I looked out into the east:
The flood of light upon the night
  Had silently increased;

The sky was pale with fervour,
  The distant trees were grey,
The hill-lines drawn like waves of dawn
  Dissolving in the day.

I looked out into the morning;
  Looked east, looked west, with glee:
O richest day of happy May,
  My Love will spend with me!

56

Ask nothing more of me, sweet;
　　All I can give you I give.
　　　Heart of my heart, were it more,
More would be laid at your feet:
　　Love that should help you to live,
　　　Song that should spur you to soar.

All things were nothing to give
　　Once to have sense of you more,
　　　Touch you and taste of you sweet,
Think you and breathe you and live,
　　Swept of your wings as they soar,
　　　Trodden by chance of your feet.

I that have love and no more
　　Give you but love of you, sweet:
　　　He that hath more, let him give;
He that hath wings, let him soar;
　　Mine is the heart at your feet
　　　Here, that must love you to live.

57

The world's gone forward to its latest fair
And dropt an old man done with by the way,
To sit alone among the bats and stare
At miles and miles and miles of moorland bare
Lit only with last shreds of dying day.

Not all the world, not all the world's gone by:
Old man, you're like to meet one traveller still,
A journeyman well kenned for courtesy
To all that walk at odds with life and limb;
If this be he now riding up the hill
Maybe he'll stop and take you up with him ...

'But thou art Death?' 'Of Heavenly Seraphim
None else to seek thee out and bid thee come.'
'I only care that thou art come from Him,
Unbody me—I'm tired—and get me home.'

58

Would some little joy to-day
　　Visit us, heart!
Could it but a moment stay,
　　Then depart,
With the flutter of its wings
Stirring sense of brighter things.

Like a butterfly astray
　　In a dark room;
Telling:—Outside there is day,
　　Sweet flowers bloom,
Birds are singing, trees are green,
Runnels ripple silver sheen.

Heart! we now have been so long
　　Sad without change,
Shut in deep from shine and song,
　　Nor can range;
It would do us good to know
That the world is not all woe.

Would some little joy to-day
　　Visit us, heart!
Could it but a moment stay,
　　Then depart,
With the lustre of its wings
Lighting dreams of happy things,
　　Oh sad my heart!

59

My young lord's the lover
　Of earth and sky above,
Of youth's sway and youth's play,
　Of songs ànd flowers and love.

My young lord's the lover
　Of every burning thought
That Love's will, that Love's skill
　Within his breast has wrought.

My young lord's the lover
　Of every tender grace
That woman, to woo man,
　Can wear in form or face.

My young lord's the lover
　Of every secret thing,
Love-hidden, love-bidden
　This day to banqueting.

And now my lord's the lover
　Of ah! so many a sweet,—
Of roses, of spouses,
　As many as love may greet.

60

Waking one morning
In a pleasant land,
By a river flowing
Over golden sand:—

Whence flow ye, waters,
O'er your golden sand?
We come flowing
From the Silent Land.

Whither flow ye, waters,
O'er your golden sand?
We go flowing
To the Silent Land.

And what is this fair realm?
A grain of golden sand
In the great darkness
Of the Silent Land.

61

Who is your lady of love, O ye that pass
Singing? and is it for sorrow of that which was
　　That ye sing sadly, or dream of what shall be?
　　　For gladly at once and sadly it seems ye sing.
— Our lady of love by you is unbeholden;
For hands she hath none, nor eyes, nor lips, nor golden
　　Treasure of hair, nor face nor form; but we
　　　That love, we know her more fair than anything.

— Is she a queen, having great gifts to give?,
— Yea, these; that whoso hath seen her shall not live
　　Except he serve her sorrowing, with strange pain,
　　　Travail and bloodshedding and bitterer tears;
And when she bids die he shall surely die.
And he shall leave all things under the sky
　　And go forth naked under sun and rain
　　　And work and wait and watch out all his years.

— Hath she on earth no place of habitation?
— Age to age calling, nation answering nation,
　　Cries out, Where is she? and there is none to say;
　　　For if she be not in the spirit of men,
For if in the inward soul she hath no place,
In vain they cry unto her, seeking her face,
　　In vain their mouths make much of her; for they
　　　Cry with vain tongues, till the heart lives again.

— O ye that follow, and have ye no repentance?
For on your brows is written a mortal sentence,
　　An hieroglyph of sorrow, a fiery sign,
　　　That in your lives ye shall not pause or rest,

Nor have the sure sweet common love, nor keep
Friends and safe days, nor joy of life nor sleep.
  —These have we not, who have one thing, the divine
    Face and clear eyes of faith and fruitful breast.

—And ye shall die before your thrones be won.
—Yea, and the changed world and the liberal sun
  Shall move and shine without us, and we lie
    Dead; but if she too move on earth and live,
But if the old world with all the old irons rent
Laugh and give thanks, shall we be not content?
  Nay, we shall rather live, we shall not die,
    Life being so little and death so good to give.

—And these men shall forget you.—Yea, but we
Shall be a part of the earth and the ancient sea,
  And heaven-high air august, and awful fire,
    And all things good; and no man's heart shall beat
But somewhat in it of our blood once shed
Shall quiver and quicken, as now in us the dead
  Blood of men slain and the old same life's desire
    Plants in their fiery footprints our fresh feet.

—But ye that might be clothed with all things pleasant,
Ye are foolish that put off the fair soft present,
  That clothe yourselves with the cold future air;
    When mother and father and tender sister and brother
And the old live love that was shall be as ye,
Dust, and no fruit of loving life shall be.
  —She shall be yet who is more than all these were,
    Than sister or wife or father unto us or mother.

—Is this worth life, is this, to win for wages?
Lo, the dead mouths of the awful grey-grown ages,
  The venerable, in the past that is their prison,
    In the outer darkness, in the unopening grave,

Laugh, knowing how many as ye now say have said,
How many, and all are fallen, are fallen and dead:
    Shall ye dead rise, and these dead have not risen?
        —Not we but she, who is tender and swift to save.

—Are ye not weary and faint not by the way,
Seeing night by night devoured of day by day,
    Seeing hour by hour consumed in sleepless fire?
        Sleepless; and ye too, when shall ye too sleep?
—We are weary in heart and head, in hands and feet,
And surely more than all things sleep were sweet,
    Than all things save the inexorable desire
        Which whoso knoweth shall neither faint nor weep.

—Is this so sweet that one were fain to follow?
Is this so sure where all men's hopes are hollow,
    Even this your dream, that by much tribulation
        Ye shall make whole flawed hearts, and bowed necks
            straight?
—Nay, though our life were blind, our death were fruitless,
Not therefore were the whole world's high hope rootless;
    But man to man, nation would turn to nation,
        And the old life live, and the old great word be great.

—Pass on then and pass by us and let us be,
For what light think ye after life to see?
    And if the world fare better will ye know?
        And if man triumph who shall seek you and say?
—Enough of light is this for one life's span,
That all men born are mortal, but not man:
    And we men bring death lives by night to sow,
        That man may reap and eat and live by day.

153

62

Weary of myself, and sick of asking
What I am, and what I ought to be,
At the vessel's prow I stand, which bears me
Forwards, forwards, o'er the starlit sea.

And a look of passionate desire
O'er the sea and to the stars I send:
'Ye who from my childhood up have calm'd me,
Calm me, ah, compose me to the end.

'Ah, once more,' I cried, 'ye Stars, ye Waters,
On my heart your mighty charm renew:
Still, still let me, as I gaze upon you,
Feel my soul becoming vast like you.'

From the intense, clear, star-sown vault of heaven,
Over the lit sea's unquiet way,
In the rustling night-air came the answer—
'Wouldst thou *be* as these are? *Live* as they.

'Unaffrighted by the silence round them,
Undistracted by the sights they see,
These demand not that the things without them
Yield them love, amusement, sympathy.

'And with joy the stars perform their shining,
And the sea its long moon-silver'd roll.
For alone they live, nor pine with noting
All the fever of some differing soul.

'Bounded by themselves, and unregardful
In what state God's other works may be,
In their own tasks all their powers pouring,
These attain the mighty life you see.'

O air-born Voice! long since, severely clear,
A cry like thine in my own heart I hear.
'Resolve to be thyself: and know, that he
Who finds himself, loses his misery.'

63

A little while a little love
   The hour yet bears for thee and me
   Who have not drawn the veil to see
If still our heaven be lit above.
Thou merely, at the day's last sigh,
   Hast felt thy soul prolong the tone;
And I have heard the night-wind cry
     And deemed its speech mine own.

A little while a little love
   The scattering autumn hoards for us
   Whose bower is not yet ruinous
Nor quite unleaved our songless grove.
Only across the shaken boughs
   We hear the flood-tides seek the sea,
And deep in both our hearts they rouse
     One wail for thee and me.

A little while a little love
   May yet be ours who have not said
   The word it makes our eyes afraid
To know that each is thinking of.
Not yet the end: be our lips dumb
   In smiles a little season yet:
I'll tell thee, when the end is come,
     How we may best forget.

64

'The Nightingale was not yet heard,
   For the Rose was not yet blown.'
His heart was quiet as a bird
   Asleep in the night alone,
And never were its pulses stirred
To breathe or joy or moan:
The Nightingale was not yet heard
   For the Rose was not yet blown.

Then She bloomed forth before his sight
   In passion and in power,
And filled the very day with light,
   So glorious was her dower;
And made the whole vast moonlit night
   As fragrant as a bower:
The young, the beautiful, the bright,
   The splendid peerless Flower.

Whereon his heart was like a bird
   When Summer mounts his throne,
And all its pulses thrilled and stirred
   To songs of joy and moan,
To every most impassioned word
   And most impassioned tone;
The Nightingale at length was heard
   For the Rose at length was blown.

65

I felt the world a-spinning on its nave,
  I felt it sheering blindly round the sun;
I felt the time had come to find a grave:
  I knew it in my heart my days were done.
I took my staff in hand; I took the road,
And wandered out to seek my last abode.
      Hearts of gold and hearts of lead
        Sing it yet in sun and rain,
      'Heel and toe from dawn to dusk,
        Round the world and home again.'

O long before the bere was steeped for malt,
  And long before the grape was crushed for wine,
The glory of the march without a halt,
  The triumph of a stride like yours and mine
Was known to folk like us, who walked about,
To be the sprightliest cordial out and out!
      Folks like us, with hearts that beat,
        Sang it too in sun and rain—
      'Heel and toe from dawn to dusk,
        Round the world and home again.'

My feet are heavy now, but on I go,
  My head erect beneath the tragic years.
The way is steep, but I would have it so;
  And dusty, but I lay the dust with tears,
Though none can see me weep: alone I climb
The rugged path that leads me out of time—
      Out of time and out of all,
        Singing yet in sun and rain,
      'Heel and toe from dawn to dusk,
        Round the world and home again.'

Farewell the hope that mocked, farewell despair
  That went before me still and made the pace.
The earth is full of graves, and mine was there
  Before my life began, my resting-place;
And I shall find it out and with the dead
Lie down for ever, all my sayings said—
    Deeds all done and songs all sung,
      While others chant in sun and rain,
    'Heel and toe from dawn to dusk,
      Round the world and home again.'

66

This is the day, which down the void abysm
At the Earth-born's spell yawns for Heaven's despotism,
   And Conquest is dragged captive through the deep:
Love, from its awful throne of patient power
In the wise heart, from the last giddy hour
   Of dread endurance, from the slippery, steep,
And narrow verge of crag-like agony, springs
And folds over the world its healing wings.

Gentleness, Virtue, Wisdom, and Endurance,
These are the seals of that most firm assurance
   Which bars the pit over Destruction's strength;
And if, with infirm hand, Eternity,
Mother of many acts and hours, should free
   The serpent that would clasp her with his length;
These are the spells by which to reassume
An empire o'er the disentangled doom.

To suffer woes which Hope thinks infinite;
To forgive wrongs darker than death or night;
   To defy Power, which seems omnipotent;
To love, and bear; to hope till Hope creates
From its own wreck the thing it contemplates;
   Neither to change, nor falter, nor repent;
This, like thy glory, Titan, is to be
Good, great and joyous, beautiful and free;
This is alone Life, Joy, Empire, and Victory.

67

These, in the day when heaven was falling,
  The hour when earth's foundations fled,
Followed their mercenary calling
  And took their wages and are dead.

Their shoulders held the sky suspended;
  They stood, and earth's foundations stay;
What God abandoned, these defended,
  And saved the sum of things for pay.

68

He stood, and heard the steeple
  Sprinkle the quarters on the morning town.
One, two, three, four, to market-place and people
  It tossed them down.

Strapped, noosed, nighing his hour,
  He stood and counted them and cursed his luck;
And then the clock collected in the tower
  Its strength, and struck.

He stood and heard the steeple
Sprinkle the quarters on the morning town,
One two, three, four, to market-place and people
It tossed them down.

Strapped, noosed, nighing his hour,
He stood and counted them, and cursed his luck:
And then the clock collected in the tower
Its strength, and struck.

69

The blessed damozel leaned out
  From the gold bar of Heaven;
Her eyes were deeper than the depth
  Of waters stilled at even;
She had three lilies in her hand,
  And the stars in her hair were seven.

Her robe, ungirt from clasp to hem,
  No wrought flowers did adorn,
But a white rose of Mary's gift,
  For service meetly worn;
Her hair that lay along her back
  Was yellow like ripe corn.

Herseemed she scarce had been a day
  One of God's choristers;
The wonder was not yet quite gone
  From that still look of hers;
Albeit, to them she left, her day
  Had counted as ten years.

(To one, it is ten years of years.
  ... Yet now, and in this place,
Surely she leaned o'er me—her hair
  Fell all about my face ...
Nothing: the autumn-fall of leaves.
  The whole year sets apace.)

It was the rampart of God's house
   That she was standing on;
By God built over the sheer depth
   The which is Space begun;
So high, that looking downward thence
   She scarce could see the sun.

It lies in Heaven, across the flood
   Of ether, as a bridge.
Beneath, the tides of day and night
   With flame and darkness ridge
The void, as low as where this earth
   Spins like a fretful midge.

Around her, lovers, newly met
   'Mid deathless love's acclaims,
Spoke evermore among themselves
   Their heart-remembered names;
And the souls mounting up to God
   Went by her like thin flames.

And still she bowed herself and stooped
   Out of the circling charm;
Until her bosom must have made
   The bar she leaned on warm,
And the lilies lay as if asleep
   Along her bended arm.

From the fixed place of Heaven she saw
   Time like a pulse shake fierce
Through all the worlds. Her gaze still strove
   Within the gulf to pierce
Its path; and now she spoke as when
   The stars sang in their spheres.

The sun was gone now; the curled moon
    Was like a little feather
Fluttering far down the gulf; and now
    She spoke through the still weather.
Her voice was like the voice the stars
    Had when they sang together.

(Ah sweet! Even now, in that bird's song,
    Strove not her accents there,
Fain to be hearkened? When those bells
    Possessed the mid-day air,
Strove not her steps to reach my side
    Down all the echoing stair?)

'I wish that he were come to me,
    For he will come,' she said.
'Have I not prayed in Heaven?—on earth,
    Lord, Lord, has he not pray'd?
Are not two prayers a perfect strength?
    And shall I feel afraid?

'When round his head the aureole clings,
    And he is clothed in white,
I'll take his hand and go with him
    To the deep wells of light;
As unto a stream we will step down,
    And bathe there in God's sight.

'We two will stand beside that shrine,
    Occult, withheld, untrod,
Whose lamps are stirred continually
    With prayer sent up to God;
And see our old prayers, granted, melt
    Each like a little cloud.

'We two will lie i' the shadow of
  That living mystic tree
Within whose secret growth the Dove
  Is sometimes felt to be,
While every leaf that His plumes touch
  Saith His Name audibly.

'And I myself will teach to him,
  I myself, lying so,
The songs I sing here; which his voice
  Shall pause in, hushed and slow,
And find some knowledge at each pause,
  Or some new thing to know.'

(Alas! we two, we two, thou say'st!
  Yea, one wast thou with me
That once of old. But shall God lift
  To endless unity
The soul whose likeness with thy soul
  Was but its love for thee?)

'We two,' she said, 'will seek the groves
  Where the lady Mary is,
With her five handmaidens, whose names
  Are five sweet symphonies,
Cecily, Gertrude, Magdalen,
  Margaret and Rosalys.

'Circlewise sit they, with bound locks
  And foreheads garlanded;
Into the fine cloth white like flame
  Weaving the golden thread,
To fashion the birth-robes for them
  Who are just born, being dead.

'He shall fear, haply, and be dumb:
  Then will I lay my cheek
To his, and tell about our love,
  Not once abashed or weak:
And the dear Mother will approve
  My pride, and let me speak.

'Herself shall bring us, hand in hand,
  To Him round whom all souls
Kneel, the clear-ranged unnumbered heads
  Bowed with their aureoles:
And angels meeting us shall sing
  To their citherns and citoles.

'There will I ask of Christ the Lord
  Thus much for him and me:—
Only to live as once on earth
  With Love,—only to be,
As then awhile, for ever now
  Together, I and he.'

She gazed and listened and then said,
  Less sad of speech than mild,—
'All this is when he comes.' She ceased.
  The light thrilled towards her, fill'd
With angels in strong level flight.
  Her eyes prayed, and she smil'd.

(I saw her smile.) But soon their path
  Was vague in distant spheres:
And then she cast her arms along
  The golden barriers,
And laid her face between her hands,
  And wept. (I heard her tears.)

70

By the waters of Babylon we sat down and wept,
   Remembering thee,
That for ages of agony hast endured, and slept,
   And wouldst not see.

By the waters of Babylon we stood up and sang,
   Considering thee,
That a blast of deliverance in the darkness rang,
   To set thee free.

And with trumpets and thunderings and with morning song
   Came up the light;
And thy spirit uplifted thee to forget thy wrong
   As day doth night.

And thy sons were dejected not any more, as then
   When thou wast shamed;
When thy lovers went heavily without heart, as men
   Whose life was maimed.

In the desolate distances, with a great desire,
   For thy love's sake,
With our hearts going back to thee, they were filled with
   fire,
   Were nigh to break.

It was said to us: 'Verily ye are great of heart,
   But ye shall bend;
Ye are bondsmen and bondswomen, to be scourged and
   smart,
   To toil and tend.'

And with harrows men harrowed us, and subdued with
    spears,
    And crushed with shame;
And the summer and winter was, and the length of years,
    And no change came.

By the rivers of Italy, by the sacred streams,
    By town, by tower,
There was feasting with revelling, there was sleep with
    dreams,
    Until thine hour.

And they slept and they rioted and their rose-hung beds,
    With mouths on flame,
And with love-locks vine-chapleted, and with rose-crowned
    heads
    And robes of shame.

And they knew not their forefathers, nor the hills and streams
    And words of power,
Nor the gods that were good to them, but with songs and
    dreams
    Filled up their hour.

By the rivers of Italy, by the dry streams' beds,
    When thy time came,
There was casting of crowns from them, from their young
    men's heads,
    The crowns of shame.

By the horn of Eridanus, by the Tiber mouth,
    As thy day rose,
They arose up and girded them to the north and south,
    By seas, by snows.

As a water in January the frost confines,
  Thy kings bound thee;
As a water in April is, in the new-blown vines,
  Thy sons made free.

And thy lovers that looked for thee, and that mourned from
    far,
  For thy sake dead,
We rejoiced in the light of thee, in the signal star
  Above thine head.

In thy grief had we followed thee, in thy passion loved,
  Loved in thy loss;
In thy shame we stood fast to thee, with thy pangs were
    moved,
  Clung to thy cross.

By the hillside of Calvary we beheld thy blood,
  Thy bloodred tears,
As a mother's in bitterness, an unebbing flood,
  Years upon years.

And the north was Gethsemane, without leaf or bloom,
  A garden sealed;
And the south was Aceldama, for a sanguine fume
  Hid all the field.

By the stone of the sepulchre we returned to weep,
  From far, from prison;
And the guards by it keeping it we beheld asleep,
  But thou wast risen.

And an angel's similitude by the unsealed grave,
  And by the stone:
And the voice was angelic, to whose words God gave
  Strength like his own.

'Lo, the graveclothes of Italy that are folded up
    In the grave's gloom!
And the guards as men wrought upon with a charmed cup,
    By the open tomb.

'And her body most beautiful, and her shining head,
    These are not here;
For your mother, for Italy, is not surely dead:
    Have ye no fear.

'As of old time she spake to you, and you hardly heard,
    Hardly took heed,
So now also she saith to you, yet another word,
    Who is risen indeed.

'By my saying she saith to you, in your ears she saith,
    Who hear these things,
Put no trust in men's royalties, nor in great men's breath,
    Nor words of kings.

'For the life of them vanishes and is no more seen,
    Nor no more known;
Nor shall any remember him if a crown hath been,
    Or where a throne.

'Unto each man his handiwork, unto each his crown,
    The just Fate gives;
Whoso takes the world's life on him and his own lays down,
    He, dying so, lives.

'Whoso bears the whole heaviness of the wronged world's
        weight
    And puts it by,
It is well with him suffering, though he face man's fate;
    How should he die?

'Seeing death has no part in him any more, no power
   Upon his head;
He has bought his eternity with a little hour,
   And is not dead.

'For an hour, if ye look for him, he is no more found,
   For one hour's space;
Then ye lift up your eyes to him and behold him crowned,
   A deathless face.

'On the mountains of memory, by the world's well-springs,
   In all men's eyes,
Where the light of the life of him is on all past things,
   Death only dies.

'Not the light that was quenched for us, nor the deeds that
      were,
   Nor the ancient days,
Nor the sorrows not sorrowful, nor the face most fair
   Of perfect praise.'

So the angel of Italy's resurrection said,
   So yet he saith;
So the son of her suffering, that from breasts nigh dead
   Drew life, not death.

That the pavement of Golgotha should be white as snow,
   Not red, but white;
That the waters of Babylon should no longer flow,
   And men see light.

71

As I went down to Dymchurch Wall,
  I heard the South sing o'er the land;
I saw the yellow sunlight fall
  On knolls where Norman churches stand.

And ringing shrilly, taut and lithe,
  Within the wind a core of sound,
The wire from Romney town to Hythe
  Alone its airy journey wound.

A veil of purple vapour flowed
  And trailed its fringe along the Straits;
The upper air like sapphire glowed;
  And roses filled Heaven's central gates.

Masts in the offing wagged their tops;
  The swinging waves pealed on the shore;
The saffron beach, all diamond drops
  And beads of surge, prolonged the roar.

As I came up from Dymchurch Wall,
  I saw above the Downs' low crest
The crimson brands of sunset fall,
  Flicker and fade from out the west.

Night sank: like flakes of silver fire
  The stars in one great shower came down;
Shrill blew the wind; and shrill the wire
  Rang out from Hythe to Romney town.

The darkly shining salt sea drops
   Streamed as the waves clashed on the shore;
The beach, with all its organ stops
   Pealing again, prolonged the roar.

72

The world's great age begins anew,
  The golden years return,
The earth doth like a snake renew
  Her winter weeds outworn:
Heaven smiles, and faiths and empires gleam,
Like wrecks of a dissolving dream.

A brighter Hellas rears its mountains
  From waves serener far;
A new Peneus rolls his fountains
  Against the morning star.
Where fairer Tempes bloom, there sleep
Young Cyclads on a sunnier deep.

A loftier Argo cleaves the main,
  Fraught with a later prize;
Another Orpheus sings again,
  And loves, and weeps, and dies.
A new Ulysses leaves once more
Calypso for his native shore.

Oh, write no more the tale of Troy,
  If earth Death's scroll must be!
Nor mix with Laian rage the joy
  Which dawns upon the free:
Although a subtler Sphinx renew
Riddles of death Thebes never knew.

Another Athens shall arise,
    And to remoter time
Bequeath, like sunset to the skies,
    The splendour of its prime;
And leave, if nought so bright may live,
All earth can take or Heaven can give.

Saturn and Love their long repose
    Shall burst, more bright and good
Than all who fell, than One who rose,
    Than many unsubdued:
Not gold, not blood, their altar dowers,
But votive tears and symbol flowers.

Oh, cease! must hate and death return?
    Cease! must men kill and die?
Cease! drain not to its dregs the urn
    Of bitter prophecy.
The world is weary of the past,
Oh, might it die or rest at last!

73

West and away the wheels of darkness roll,
  Day's beamy banner up the east is borne,
Spectres and fears, the nightmare and her foal,
  Drown in the golden deluge of the morn.

But over sea and continent from sight
  Safe to the Indies has the earth conveyed
The vast and moon-eclipsing cone of night,
  Her towering foolscap of eternal shade.

See, in mid heaven the sun is mounted; hark,
  The belfries tingle to the noonday chime.
'Tis silent, and the subterranean dark
  Has crossed the nadir, and begins to climb.

74

The sun is warm, the sky is clear,
   The waves are dancing fast and bright,
Blue isles and snowy mountains wear
   The purple noon's transparent might,
   The breath of the moist earth is light,
Around its unexpanded buds;
   Like many a voice of one delight,
The winds, the birds, the ocean floods,
The City's voice itself, is soft like Solitude's.

I see the Deep's untrampled floor
   With green and purple seaweeds strown;
I see the waves upon the shore,
   Like light dissolved in star-showers, thrown:
   I sit upon the sands alone,—
The lightning of the noontide ocean
   Is flashing round me, and a tone
Arises from its measured motion,
How sweet! did any heart now share in my emotion.

Alas! I have nor hope nor health,
   Nor peace within nor calm around,
Nor that content surpassing wealth
   The sage in meditation found,
   And walked with inward glory crowned—
Nor fame, nor power, nor love, nor leisure.
   Others I see whom these surround—
Smiling they live, and call life pleasure;—
To me that cup has been dealt in another measure.

Yet now despair itself is mild,
  Even as the winds and waters are;
I could lie down like a tired child,
  And weep away the life of care
  Which I have borne and yet must bear,
Till death like sleep might steal on me,
  And I might feel in the warm air
My cheek grow cold, and hear the sea
Breathe o'er my dying brain its last monotony.

Some might lament that I were cold,
  As I, when this sweet day is gone,
Which my lost heart, too soon grown old,
  Insults with this untimely moan;
  They might lament—for I am one
Whom men love not,—and yet regret,
  Unlike this day, which, when the sun
Shall on its stainless glory set,
Will linger, though enjoyed, like joy in memory yet.

75

'Who rules these lands?' the Pilgrim said.
  'Stranger, Queen Blanchelys.'
'And who has thus harried them?' he said.
  'It was Duke Luke did this:
    God's ban be his!'

The Pilgrim said: 'Where is your house?
  I'll rest there, with your will.'
'You've but to climb these blackened boughs
  And you'll see it over the hill,
    For it burns still.'

'Which road, to seek your Queen?' said he.
  'Nay, nay, but with some wound
You'll fly back hither, it may be,
  And by your blood i' the ground
    My place be found.'

'Friend, stay in peace. God keep your head,
  And mine, where I will go;
For He is here and there,' he said.
  He passed the hill-side, slow,
    And stood below.

The Queen sat idle by her loom:
  She heard the arras stir,
And looked up sadly: through the room
  The sweetness sickened her
    Of musk and myrrh.

Her women, standing two and two,
    In silence combed the fleece.
The Pilgrim said, 'Peace be with you,
    Lady;' and bent his knees.
        She answered, 'Peace.'

Her eyes were like the wave within;
    Like water-reeds the poise
Of her soft body, dainty thin;
    And like the water's noise
        Her plaintive voice.

For him, the stream had never well'd
    In desert tracks malign
So sweet; nor had he ever felt
    So faint in the sunshine
        Of Palestine.

Right so, he knew that he saw weep
    Each night through every dream
The Queen's own face, confused in sleep
    With visages supreme
        Not known to him.

'Lady,' he said, 'your lands lie burnt
    And waste: to meet your foe
All fear: this I have seen and learnt.
    Say that it shall be so,
        And I will go.'

She gazed at him. 'Your cause is just,
    For I have heard the same,'
He said: 'God's strength shall be my trust.
    Fall it to good or grame,
        'Tis in His name.'

'Sir, you are thanked. My cause is dead.
　　Why should you toil to break
A grave, and fall therein?' she said.
　　He did not pause but spake:
　　　'For my vow's sake.'

'Can such vows be, Sir—to God's ear,
　　Not to God's will?' 'My vow
Remains: God heard me there as here,'
　　He said with reverent brow,
　　　'Both then and now.'

They gazed together, he and she,
　　The minute while he spoke;
And when he ceased, she suddenly
　　Looked round upon her folk
　　　As though she woke.

'Fight, Sir,' she said; 'my prayers in pain
　　Shall be your fellowship.'
He whispered one among her train,—
　　'To-morrow bid her keep
　　　This staff and scrip.'

She sent him a sharp sword, whose belt
　　About his body there
As sweet as her own arms he felt.
　　He kissed its blade, all bare,
　　　Instead of her.

She sent him a green banner wrought
　　With one white lily stem,
To bind his lance with when he fought.
　　He writ upon the same
　　　And kissed her name.

She sent him a white shield, whereon
  She bade that he should trace
His will. He blent fair hues that shone,
  And in a golden space
    He kissed her face.

Born of the day that died, that eve
  Now dying sank to rest;
As he, in likewise taking leave,
  Once with a heaving breast
    Looked to the west.

And there the sunset skies unseal'd,
  Like lands he never knew,
Beyond to-morrow's battle-field
  Lay open out of view
    To ride into.

Next day till dark the women pray'd:
  Nor any might know there
How the fight went: the Queen has bade
  That there do come to her
    No messenger.

The Queen is pale, her maidens ail;
  And to the organ-tones
They sing but faintly, who sang well
  The matin-orisons,
    The lauds and nones.

Lo, Father, is thine ear inclin'd,
  And hath thine angel pass'd?
For these thy watchers now are blind
  With vigil, and at last
    Dizzy with fast.

Weak now to them the voice o' the priest
　　As any trance affords;
And when each anthem failed and ceas'd,
　　It seemed that the last chords
　　　　Still sang the words.

'Oh what is the light that shines so red?
　　'Tis long since the sun set;'
Quoth the youngest to the eldest maid:
　　''Twas dim but now, and yet
　　　　The light is great.'

Quoth the other: ''Tis our sight is dazed
　　That we see flame i' the air.'
But the Queen held her brows and gazed,
　　And said, 'It is the glare
　　　　Of torches there.'

'Oh what are the sounds that rise and spread?
　　All day it was so still;'
Quoth the youngest to the eldest maid:
　　'Unto the furthest hill
　　　　The air they fill.'

Quoth the other: ''Tis our sense is blurr'd
　　With all the chants gone by.'
But the Queen held her breath and heard,
　　And said, 'It is the cry
　　　　Of Victory.'

The first of all the rout was sound,
　　The next were dust and flame,
And then the horses shook the ground:
　　And in the thick of them
　　　　A still band came.

'Oh what do ye bring out of the fight,
    Thus hid beneath these boughs?'
'Thy conquering guest returns to-night,
    And yet shall not carouse,
        Queen, in thy house.'

'Uncover ye his face,' she said.
    'O changed in little space!'
She cried, 'O pale that was so red!
    O God, O God of grace!
        Cover his face.'

His sword was broken in his hand
    Where he had kissed the blade.
'O soft steel that could not withstand!
    O my hard heart unstayed,
        That prayed and prayed!'

His bloodied banner crossed his mouth
    Where he had kissed her name.
'O east, and west, and north, and south,
    Fair flew my web, for shame,
        To guide Death's aim!'

The tints were shredded from his shield
    Where he had kissed her face.
'Oh, of all gifts that I could yield,
    Death only keeps its place,
        My gift and grace!'

Then stepped a damsel to her side,
    And spoke, and needs must weep:
'For his sake, lady, if he died,
    He prayed of thee to keep
        This staff and scrip.'

That night they hung above her bed,
   Till morning wet with tears.
Year after year above her head
   Her bed his token wears,
     Five years, ten years.

That night the passion of her grief
   Shook them as there they hung.
Each year the wind that shed the leaf
   Shook them and in its tongue
     A message flung.

And once she woke with a clear mind
   That letters writ to calm
Her soul lay in the scrip; to find
   Only a torpid balm
     And dust of palm.

They shook far off with palace sport
   When joust and dance were rife;
And the hunt shook them from the court;
   For hers, in peace or strife,
     Was a Queen's life.

A Queen's death now: as now they shake
   To gusts in chapel dim,—
Hung where she sleeps, not seen to wake,
   (Carved lovely white and slim),
     With them by him.

Stand up to-day, still armed, with her,
   Good knight, before His brow
Who then as now was here and there,
   Who had in mind thy vow
     Then even as now.

The lists are set in Heaven to-day,
    The bright pavilions shine;
Fair hangs thy shield, and none gainsay;
    The trumpets sound in sign
        That she is thine.

Not tithed with days' and years' decease
    He pays thy wage He owed,
But with imperishable peace
    Here in His own abode,
        Thy jealous God.

76

Foxes peeped from out their dens;
  Day grew pale and olden;
Blackbirds, willow-warblers, wrens
  Staunched their voices golden.

High, oh high, from the opal sky,
  Shouting against the dark,
'Why, why, why must the day go by?'
  Fell a passionate lark.

But the cuckoos beat their brazen gongs,
  Sounding, sounding, so;
And the nightingales poured in starry songs
  A galaxy below.

Slowly tolling, the vesper bell
  Ushered the shadowy night:
Down-a-down in a hawthorn dell
  A boy and a girl and love's delight.

By lichened tree and mossy plinth
  Like living flames of purple fire,
Flooding the wood, the hyacinth
  Uprears its heavy-scented spire.

The redstart shakes its crimson plume,
  Singing alone till evening's fall
Beside the pied and homely bloom
  Of wallflower on the crumbling wall.

Now dandelions light the way,
  Expecting summer's near approach;
And, bearing lanterns night and day,
  The great marsh-marigolds keep watch.

77

I bring fresh showers for the thirsting flowers,
    From the seas and the streams;
I bear light shade for the leaves when laid
    In their noonday dreams.
From my wings are shaken the dews that waken
    The sweet buds every one,
When rocked to rest on their mother's breast,
    As she dances about the sun.
I wield the flail of the lashing hail,
    And whiten the green plains under,
And then again I dissolve it in rain,
    And laugh as I pass in thunder.

I sift the snow on the mountains below,
    And their great pines groan aghast;
And all the night 'tis my pillow white,
    While I sleep in the arms of the blast.
Sublime on the towers of my skiey bowers,
    Lightning my pilot sits;
In a cavern under is fettered the thunder,
    It struggles and howls at fits;
    Over earth and ocean, with gentle motion,
    This pilot is guiding me,
Lured by the love of the genii that move
    In the depth of the purple sea;
Over the rills, and the crags, and the hills,
    Over the lakes and the plains,
Wherever he dream, under mountain or stream,
    The Spirit he loves remains;
And I all the while bask in Heaven's blue smile,
    Whilst he is dissolving in rains.

The sanguine Sunrise, with his meteor eyes,
    And his burning plumes outspread,
Leaps on the back of my sailing rack,
    When the morning star shines dead;
As on the jag of a mountain crag,
    Which an earthquake rocks and swings,
An eagle alit one moment may sit
    In the light of its golden wings.
And when Sunset may breathe, from the lit sea beneath,
    Its ardours of rest and of love,
And the crimson pall of eve may fall
    From the depth of Heaven above,
With wings folded I rest, on mine aëry nest,
    As still as a brooding dove.

That orbèd maiden with white fire laden,
    Whom mortals call the Moon,
Glides glimmering o'er my fleece-like floor,
    By the midnight breezes strewn;
And wherever the beat of her unseen feet,
    Which only the angels hear,
May have broken the woof of my tent's thin roof,
    The stars peep behind her and peer;
And I laugh to see them whirl and flee,
    Like a swarm of golden bees,
When I widen the rent in my wind-built tent,
    Till the calm rivers, lakes, and seas,
Like strips of the sky fallen through me on high,
    Are each paved with the moon and these.

I bind the Sun's throne with a burning zone,
    And the Moon's with a girdle of pearl;
The volcanoes are dim, and the stars reel and swim,
    When the whirlwinds my banner unfurl.
From cape to cape, with a bridge-like shape,
    Over a torrent sea,

Sunbeam-proof, I hang like a roof,—
    The mountains its columns be.
The triumphal arch through which I march
    With hurricane, fire, and snow,
When the Powers of the air are chained to my chair,
    Is the million-coloured bow;
The sphere-fire above its soft colours wove,
    While the moist Earth was laughing below.

I am the daughter of Earth and Water,
    And the nursling of the Sky;
I pass through the pores of the ocean and shores;
    I change, but I cannot die.
For after the rain when with never a stain
    The pavilion of Heaven is bare,
And the winds and sunbeams with their convex gleams
    Build up the blue dome of air,
I silently laugh at my own cenotaph,
    And out of the caverns of rain,
Like a child from the womb, like a ghost from the tomb,
    I arise and unbuild it again.

78

I sat in a friendly company
And wagged my wicked tongue so well,
My friends were listening close to hear
The wickedest tales that I could tell.
For many a fond youth waits, I said,
On many a worthless damozel;
But every trusting fool shall learn
To wish them heartily in hell.

And when your name was spoken too,
I did not change, I did not start,
And when they only praised and loved,
I still could play my secret part,
Cursing and lies upon my tongue,
And songs and shouting in my heart.

But when you came and looked at me,
You tried my poor pretence too much.
O love, do you know the secret now
Of one who would not tell nor touch?
Must I confess before the pack
Of babblers, idiots, and such?

Do they not hear the burst of bells,
Pealing at every step you make?
Are not their eyelids winking too,
Feeling your sudden brightness break?
O too much glory shut with us!
O walls too narrow and opaque!
O come into the night with me
And let me speak, for Jesus' sake.

79

When the words rustle no more,
   And the last work's done,
When the bolt lies deep in the door,
   And Fire, our Sun,
Falls on the dark-laned meadows of the floor;

When from the clock's last chime to the next chime
   Silence beats his drum,
And Space with gaunt grey eyes and her brother Time
   Wheeling and whispering come,
She with the mould of form and he with the loom of rhyme:

Then twittering out in the night my thought-birds flee,
   I am emptied of all my dreams:
I only hear Earth turning, only see
   Ether's long ·bankless streams,
And only know I should drown if you laid not your hand
   on me.

80

We who are old, old and gay,
O so old!
Thousands of years, thousands of years,
If all were told:

Give to these children, new from the world,
Silence and love;
And the long dew-dropping hours of the night,
And the stars above:

Give to these children, new from the world,
Rest far from men.
Is anything better, anything better?
Tell us it then:

Us who are old, old and gay,
O so old!
Thousands of years, thousands of years,
If all were told.

81

Now first, as I shut the door,
   I was alone
In the new house; and the wind
   Began to moan.

Old at once was the house,
   And I was old;
My ears were teased with the dread
   Of what was foretold,

Nights of storm, days of mist, without end;
   Sad days when the sun
Shone in vain: old griefs and griefs
   Not yet begun.

All was foretold me; naught
   Could I foresee;
But I learned how the wind would sound
   After these things should be.

82

'What have you looked at, Moon,
      In your time,
   Now long past your prime?'
'O, I have looked at, often looked at
      Sweet, sublime,
Sore things, shudderful, night and noon
      In my time.'

   'What have you mused on, Moon,
      In your day,
   So aloof, so far away?'
'O, I have mused on, often mused on
      Growth, decay,
Nations alive, dead, mad, aswoon,
      In my day!'

   'Have you much wondered, Moon,
      On your rounds,
   Self-wrapt, beyond Earth's bounds?'
'Yea, I have wondered, often wondered
      At the sounds
Reaching me of the human tune
      On my rounds.'

   'What do you think of it, Moon,
      As you go?
   Is Life much, or no?'
'O, I think of it, often think of it
      As a show
God means surely to shut up soon,
      As I go.'

83

Far are the shades of Arabia,
    Where the Princes ride at noon,
'Mid the verdurous vales and thickets,
    Under the ghost of the moon;
And so dark is that vaulted purple
    Flowers in the forest rise
And toss into blossom 'gainst the phantom stars
    Pale in the noonday skies.

Sweet is the music of Arabia
    In my heart, when out of dreams
I still in the thin clear mirk of dawn
    Descry her gliding streams;
Hear her strange lutes on the green banks
    Ring loud with the grief and delight
Of the dim-silked, dark-haired Musicians
    In the brooding silence of night.

They haunt me—her lutes and her forests;
    No beauty on earth I see
But shadowed with that dreams recalls
    Her loveliness to me:
Still eyes look coldly upon me,
    Cold voices whisper and say—
'He is crazed with the spell of far Arabia,
    They have stolen his wits away.'

84

We swing ungirded hips,
And lightened are our eyes,
The rain is on our lips,
We do not run for prize.
We know not whom we trust
Nor whitherward we fare,
But we run because we must
   Through the great wide air.

The waters of the seas
Are troubled as by storm.
The tempest strips the trees
And does not leave them warm.
Does the tearing tempest pause?
Do the tree-tops ask it why?
So we run without a cause
   'Neath the big bare sky.

The rain is on our lips,
We do not run for prize.
But the storm the water whips
And the wave howls to the skies.
The winds arise and strike it
And scatter it like sand,
And we run because we like it
   Through the broad bright land.

85

I will arise and go now, and go to Innisfree,
And a small cabin build there, of clay and wattles made:
Nine bean-rows will I have there, a hive for the honey-bee,
And live alone in the bee-loud glade.

And I shall have some peace there, for peace comes dropping
    slow,
Dropping from the veils of the morning to where the cricket
    sings;
There midnight's all a glimmer, and noon a purple glow,
And evening full of the linnet's wings.

I will arise and go now, for always night and day
I hear lake water lapping with low sounds by the shore;
While I stand on the roadway, or on the pavements grey,
I hear it in the deep heart's core.

86

Of Love he sang, full-hearted one.
But when the song was done
The King demanded more,
Ay, and commanded more.
The boy found nothing for encore,
Words, melodies, none:
Ashamed the song's glad rise and plaintive fall
Had so charmed King and Queen and all.

He sang the same verse once again,
But urging less Love's pain,
With altered time and key
He showed variety,
Seemed to refresh the harmony
Of his only strain,
So still the glad rise and the plaintive fall
Could charm the King, the Queen, and all.

He of his song then wearying ceased,
But was not yet released;
The Queen's request was *More*,
And her behest was *More*.
He played of random notes some score,
He found his rhymes at least—
Then suddenly let his twangling harp down fall
And fled in tears from King and Queen and all.

87

In this way I,

With sleepy face bent to the chapel floor,
   Kept musing half asleep, till suddenly
A sharp bell rang from close beside the door,
   And I leapt up when something pass'd me by,

Shrill ringing going with it, still half blind
   I stagger'd after, a great sense of awe
At every step kept gathering on my mind,
   Thereat I have no marvel, for I saw

One sitting on the altar as a throne,
   Whose face no man could say he did not know,
And though the bell still rang, he sat alone,
   With raiment half blood-red, half white as snow.

Right so I fell upon the floor and knelt,
   Not as one kneels in church when mass is said,
But in a heap, quite nerveless, for I felt
   The first time what a thing was perfect dread.

But mightily the gentle voice came down:
   'Rise up, and look and listen, Galahad,
Good knight of God, for you will see no frown
   Upon my face; I come to make you glad.

'For that you say that you are all alone,
   I will be with you always, and fear not
You are uncared for, though no maiden moan
   Above your empty tomb; for Launcelot,

'He in good time shall be my servant too,
   Meantime, take note whose sword first made him knight,
And who has loved him alway, yea, and who
   Still trusts him alway, though in all men's sight,

'He is just what you know, O Galahad;
   This love is happy even as you say,
But would you for a little time be glad,
   To make ME sorry long day after day?

'Her warm arms round his neck half throttle ME,
   The hot love-tears burn deep like spots of lead,
Yea, and the years pass quick: right dismally
   Will Launcelot at one time hang his head;

'Yea, old and shrivell'd he shall win my love.
   Poor Palomydes fretting out his soul!
Not always is he able, son, to move
   His love, and do it honour: needs must roll

'The proudest destrier sometimes in the dust,
   And then 'tis weary work; he strives beside
Seem better than he is, so that his trust
   Is always on what chances may betide;

'And so he wears away, my servant, too,
   When all these things are gone, and wretchedly
He sits and longs to moan for Iseult, who
   Is no care now to Palomydes: see,

'O good son Galahad, upon this day,
   Now even, all these things are on your side,
But these you fight not for; look up, I say,
   And see how I can love you, for no pride

'Closes your eyes, no vain lust keeps them down.
   See now you have ME always; following
That holy vision, Galahad, go on,
   Until at last you come to ME to sing

'In Heaven always, and to walk around
   The garden where I am.'

88

When I set out for Lyonnesse,
  A hundred miles away,
  The rime was on the spray,
And starlight lit my lonesomeness
When I set out for Lyonnesse
  A hundred miles away.

What would bechance at Lyonnesse
  While I should sojourn there
  No prophet durst declare,
Nor did the wisest wizard guess
What would bechance at Lyonnesse
  While I should sojourn there.

When I came back from Lyonnesse
  With magic in my eyes,
  All marked with mute surmise
My radiance rare and fathomless,
When I came back from Lyonnesse
  With magic in my eyes.

89

Mysterious Night! when our first parent knew
Thee from report divine, and heard thy name,
Did he not tremble for this lovely frame,
This glorious canopy of light and blue?

Yet 'neath a curtain of translucent dew,
Bathed in the rays of the great setting flame,
Hesperus with the host of heaven came,
And lo! Creation widened in man's view.

Who could have thought such darkness lay concealed
Within thy beams, O sun! or who could find,
Whilst fly and leaf and insect stood revealed,
That to such countless orbs thou mad'st us blind!

Mysterious Night! when our first parent knew
Thee from report divine, and heard thy name,
Did he not tremble for this lovely frame,
This glorious canopy of light and blue?

Yet 'neath a curtain of translucent dew,
Bathed in the rays of the great setting flame,
Hesperus with the host of heaven came
And lo! Creation widened in man's view.

Who could have thought such darkness lay concealed
Within thy beams, O Sun! or who could find,
Whilst flower and leaf and insect stood revealed,
That to such countless orbs thou mad'st us blind!

90

Ah no, not these!
These, who were childless, are not they who gave
So many dead unto the journeying wave,
The helpless nurslings of the cradling seas;
Not they who doomed by infallible decrees
Unnumbered man to the innumerable grave.

But those who slay
Are fathers. Theirs are armies. Death is theirs,
The death of innocences and despairs;
The dying of the golden and the grey.
The sentence, when these speak it, has no Nay.
And she who slays is she who bears, who bears.

91

How sweet I roam'd from field to field
And tasted all the summer's pride,
Till I the Prince of Love beheld
Who in the sunny beams did glide!

He show'd me lilies for my hair,
And blushing roses for my brow;
He led me through his gardens fair
Where all his golden pleasures grow.

With sweet May dews my wings were wet,
And Phoebus fir'd my golden rage;
He caught me in his silken net,
And shut me in his golden cage.

He loves to sit and hear me sing,
Then, laughing, sports and plays with me;
Then stretches out my golden wing,
And mocks my loss of liberty.

92

I know a little garden-close
Set thick with lily and red rose,
Where I would wander if I might
From dewy dawn to dewy night,
And have one with me wandering.

And though within it no birds sing,
And though no pillar'd house is there,
And though the apple boughs are bare
Of fruit and blossom, would to God,
Her feet upon the green grass trod,
And I beheld them as before!

There comes a murmur from the shore,
And in the place two fair streams are,
Drawn from the purple hills afar,
Drawn down unto the restless sea;
The hills whose flowers ne'er fed the bee,
The shore no ship has ever seen,
Still beaten by the billows green,
Whose murmur comes unceasingly
Unto the place for which I cry.

For which I cry both day and night,
For which I let slip all delight,
That maketh me both deaf and blind,
Careless to win, unskill'd to find,
And quick to lose what all men seek.

Yet tottering as I am, and weak,
Still have I left a little breath
To seek within the jaws of death
An entrance to that happy place;
To seek the unforgotten face
Once seen, once kiss'd, once reft from me
Anigh the murmuring of the sea.

93

I longed to love a full-boughed beech
   And be as high as he:
I stretched an arm within his reach,
   And signalled unity.
But with his drip he forced a breach,
   And tried to poison me.

I gave the grasp of partnership
   To one of other race—
A plane: he barked him strip by strip
   From upper bough to base;
And me therewith; for gone my grip,
   My arms could not enlace.

In new affection next I strove
   To coll an ash I saw,
And he in trust received my love;
   Till with my soft green claw
I cramped and bound him as I wove ...
   Such was my love: ha-ha!

By this I gained his strength and height
   Without his rivalry.
But in my triumph I lost sight
   Of afterhaps. Soon he,
Being bark-bound, flagged, snapped, fell outright,
   And in his fall felled me!

94

And did those feet in ancient time
  Walk upon England's mountains green?
And was the holy Lamb of God
  On England's pleasant pastures seen?

And did the Countenance Divine
  Shine forth upon our clouded hills?
And was Jerusalem builded here
  Among these dark Satanic Mills?

Bring me my bow of burning gold!
  Bring me my arrows of desire!
Bring me my spear! O clouds, unfold!
  Bring me my chariot of fire!

I will not cease from mental fight,
  Nor shall my sword sleep in my hand,
Till we have built Jerusalem
  In England's green and pleasant land.

And did those feet in ancient time
    Walk upon England's mountain green?
And was the holy Lamb of God
    On England's pleasant pasture seen?

And did the countenance divine
    Shine forth upon our clouded hills?
And was Jerusalem builded here
    Among these dark Satanic mills?

Bring me my bow of burning gold,
    Bring me my arrows of desire,
Bring me my spear, O clouds, unfold!
    Bring me my chariot of fire!

I will not cease from mental fight,
    Nor shall my sword sleep in my hand,
Till we have built Jerusalem
    In England's green and pleasant land.

95

Give me my scallop-shell of quiet,
    My staff of faith to walk upon,
My scrip of joy, immortal diet,
    My bottle of salvation,
My gown of glory, hope's true gage;
And thus I'll take my pilgrimage.

Blood must be my body's balmer;
    No other balm will there be given;
Whilst my soul, like quiet palmer,
    Travelleth towards the land of heaven;
Over the silver mountains,
Where spring the nectar fountains:
        There will I kiss
        The bowl of bliss;
        And drink mine everlasting fill
        Upon every milken hill.
        My soul will be a-dry before;
        But, after, it will thirst no more.

96

Ah! no, no, it is nothing, surely nothing at all,
Only the wild-going wind round by the garden-wall,
For the dawn just now is breaking, the wind beginning to fall.

> *Wind, wind! thou art sad, art thou kind?*
> *Wind, wind, unhappy! thou art blind,*
> *Yet still thou wanderest the lily-seed to find.*

So I will sit, and think and think of the days gone by,
Never moving my chair for fear the dogs should cry,
Making no noise at all while the flambeau burns awry.
For my chair is heavy and carved, and with sweeping green
behind
It is hung, and the dragons thereon grin out in the gusts of
the wind;
On its folds an orange lies, with a deep gash cut in the rind.

> *Wind, wind! thou art sad, art thou kind?*
> *Wind, wind, unhappy! thou art blind,*
> *Yet still thou wanderest the lily-seed to find.*

If I move my chair it will scream, and the orange will roll
out far,
And the faint yellow juice ooze out like blood from a
wizard's jar;
And the dogs will howl for those who went last month to
the war.

> *Wind, wind! thou art sad, art thou kind?*
> *Wind, wind, unhappy! thou art blind,*
> *Yet still thou wanderest the lily-seed to find.*

.   .   .   .   .

I shriek'd and leapt from my chair, and the orange roll'd out
    far,
The faint yellow juice oozed out like blood from a wizard's
    jar;
And then in march'd the ghosts of those that had gone to the
    war.
I knew them by the arms that I was used to paint
Upon their long thin shields; but the colours were all grown
    faint,
And faint upon their banner was Olaf, king and saint.

Wind, wind! thou art sad, art thou kind?
Wind, wind, unhappy! thou art blind,
Yet still thou wanderest the lily-seed to find.

97

Last as first the question rings
Of the Will's long travailings;
    Why the All-mover,
    Why the All-prover
Ever urges on and measures out the chordless chime of Things.

Heaving dumbly
As we deem,
Moulding numbly
As in dream,
Apprehending not how fare the sentient subjects of Its scheme.

Nay;—shall not Its blindness break?
Yea, must not Its heart awake,
    Promptly tending
    To Its mending
In a genial germing purpose, and for loving-kindness' sake?

Should It never
Curb or cure
Aught whatever
Those endure
Whom It quickens, let them darkle to extinction swift and
  sure.

But—a stirring thrills the air
Like to sounds of joyance there
    That the rages
    Of the ages

Shall be cancelled, and deliverance offered from the darts that were,
Consciousness the Will informing, till It fashion all things fair!

Last as first the question rings
Of the Will's long travailings;
    Why the All-Mover,
    Why the All-Prover
Ever urges on and measures out the chordless chime of Things.

    Hearing dumbly
    As we deem,
    Moulding numbly
    As in dream,
Apprehending not how fare the sentient subjects of Its scheme.

    Nay:— shall not Its blindness break?
    Yea, must not Its heart awake,
      Promptly tending
      To Its mending
In a genial germing purpose, and for loving-kindness' sake?

    Should It never
    Curb or cure
    Aught whatever
    Those endure
Whom It quickens, let them darkle to extinction swift and sure.

    But — a stirring thrills the air
    Like to sounds of joyance there
      That the rages
      Of the ages
Shall be cancelled, and deliverance offered from the darts that were,
Consciousness the Will informing, till It fashion all things fair!

98

One thing I craved, one thing you would not grant me—
    (Oh, nothing you *could* give me, you denied)—
Your love's for others. Yet they shall not supplant me:
    Others—they, too, shall pass unsatisfied.

I craved your love. And what you could, you gave me,
    Your body's beauty; yet I sought the soul.
Not loving me, dear child, you could not save me:
    Yet all your love could not have made me whole.

For thus men's hearts have ached since man's beginning;
    Beauty can blast, Love cannot wholly bless.
We stretch vain hands—pure hands alike and sinning;
    But Beauty cannot give, nor Love possess.

As, in old tales, when wraiths of lovers perished
    Glimmered once more on eyes that wept them dead,
Still from the living arms that vainly cherished,
    A smoke, a dream, the subtle phantom fled;

So, love, I love not you but what I dream you,
    My soul grows sick with clutching at a shade.
Let others seem to win the shapes that seem you:
    Only our pain is never masquerade.

99

I hear a sudden cry of pain!
There is a rabbit in a snare:
Now I hear the cry again,
But I cannot tell from where.

But I cannot tell from where
He is calling out for aid!
Crying on the frightened air,
Making everything afraid!

Making everything afraid!
Wrinkling up his little face!
As he cries again for aid;
—And I cannot find the place!

And I cannot find the place
Where his paw is in the snare!
Little One! Oh, Little One!
I am searching everywhere!

100

Sweep thy faint strings, Musician,
  With thy long lean hand;
Downward the starry tapers burn,
  Sinks soft the waning sand;
The old hound whimpers couched in sleep,
  The embers smoulder low;
Across the walls the shadows
    Come, and go.

Sweep softly thy strings, Musician,
  The minutes mount to hours;
Frost on the windless casement weaves
  A labyrinth of flowers;
Ghosts linger in the darkening air,
  Hearken at the open door;
Music hath called them, dreaming,
    Home once more.

101

The woods and downs have caught the mid-December,
   The noisy woods and high sea-downs of home;
The wind has found me and I do remember
·   The strong scent of the foam.

The Channel is up, the little seas are leaping,
   The tide is making over Arun Bar;
And there's my boat, where all the rest are sleeping
   And my companions are.

Now shall I drive her, roaring hard a' weather,
   Right for the salt and leave them all behind.
We'll quite forget the treacherous streets together
   And find—or shall we find?

There is no Pilotry my soul relies on
   Whereby to catch beneath my bended hand,
Faint and beloved along the extreme horizon
   That unforgotten land.

We shall not round the granite piers and paven
   To lie to wharves we know with canvas furled.
My little Boat, we shall not make the haven—
   It is not of the world.

Somewhere of English forelands grandly guarded
   It stands, but not for exiles, marked and clean;
Oh! not for us. A mist has risen and marred it:—
   My youth lies in between.

102

I have come to the borders of sleep,
The unfathomable deep
Forest where all must lose
Their way, however straight,
Or winding, soon or late;
They cannot choose.

Many a road and track
That, since the dawn's first crack,
Up to the forest brink,
Deceived the travellers,
Suddenly now blurs,
And in they sink.

Here love ends,
Despair, ambition ends,
All pleasure and all trouble,
Although most sweet or bitter,
Here ends in sleep that is sweeter
Than tasks most noble.

There is not any book
Or face of dearest look
That I would not turn from now
To go into the unknown
I must enter and leave alone
I know not how.

The tall forest towers;
Its cloudy foliage lowers
Ahead, shelf above shelf;
Its silence I hear and obey
That I may lose my way
And myself.

103

'Swerve to the left, son Roger,' he said,
   'When you catch his eyes through the helmet-slit,
Swerve to the left, then out at his head,
   And the Lord God give you joy of it!'

The blue owls on my father's hood
   Were a little dimm'd as I turn'd away;
This giving up of blood for blood
   Will finish here somehow to-day.

So—when I walk'd out from the tent,
   Their howling almost blinded me;
Yet for all that I was not bent
   By any shame. Hard by, the sea

Made a noise like the aspens where
   We did that wrong, but now the place
Is very pleasant, and the air
   Blows cool on any passer's face.

And all the wrong is gather'd now
   Into the circle of these lists—
Yea, howl out, butchers! tell me how
   His hands were cut off at the wrists;

And how Lord Roger bore his face
   A league above his spear-point, high
Above the owls, to that strong place
   Among the waters—yea, yea, cry:

"Swerve to the left, son Roger," he said
"When you catch his eyes through the helmet-slit,
Swerve to the left, then out at his head,
And the Lord God give you joy of it!"
The blue owls on my father's hood
Were a little dimmed as I turned away;
This giving up of blood for blood
Will finish here somehow to-day.

So — when I walked out from the tent,
Their howling almost blinded me;
Yet for all that I was not bent
By any shame. Hard by the sea
Made a noise like the aspens where
We did that wrong, but now the place
Is very pleasant, and the air
Blows cool on any passer's face.

And all the wrong is gathered now
Into the circle of these lists —
Yea, howl out, butchers! tell me how
His hands were cut off at the wrists;
And how Lord Roger bore his face
A league above his spear-point high
Above the owls, to that strong place
Among the waters — yea, yea, cry:

"What a brave champion we have got!
Sir Oliver, the flower of all
The Hainault knights!" The day being hot,
He sat beneath a broad white pall,
White linen over all no steel:
What a good knight he looked! his sword
Laid thwart his knees; he liked to feel
Its steel edge clear as his word.
And he looked solemn: how his love
Smiled whitely on him, sick with fear!
How all the ladies up 'above
Twisted their pretty hands! so near

The fighting was — Ellayne! Ellayne!
They cannot love like you can, who
Would burn your hands off, if that pain
Could win a kiss — am I not true

To you for ever? therefore I
Do not fear death or anything;
If I should limp home wounded, why,
While I lay sick you would but sing,

'What a brave champion we have got!
    Sir Oliver, the flower of all
The Hainault knights!' The day being hot,
    He sat beneath a broad white pall,

White linen over all his steel;
    What a good knight he look'd! his sword
Laid thwart his knees; he liked to feel
    Its steadfast edge clear as his word.

And he look'd solemn; how his love
    Smiled whitely on him, sick with fear!
How all the ladies up above
    Twisted their pretty hands! so near

The fighting was—Ellayne! Ellayne!
    They cannot love like you can, who
Would burn your hands off, if that pain
    Could win a kiss—am I not true

To you for ever? therefore I
    Do not fear death or anything;
If I should limp home wounded, why,
    While I lay sick you would but sing,

And soothe me into quiet sleep.
    If they spat on the recreaunt knight,
Threw stones at him, and cursed him deep,
    Why then—what then; your hand would light

So gently on his drawn-up face,
    And you would kiss him, and in soft
Cool scented clothes would lap him, pace
    The quiet room and weep oft,—oft

Would turn and smile, and brush his cheek
 With your sweet chin and mouth; and in
The order'd garden you would seek
 The biggest roses—any sin.

And these say: 'No more now my knight,
 Or God's knight any longer'—you,
Being than they so much more white,
 So much more pure and good and true,

Will cling to me for ever—there,
 Is not that wrong turn'd right at last
Through all these years, and I wash'd clean?
 Say, yea, Ellayne; the time is past,

Since on that Christmas-day last year
 Up to your feet the fire crept,
And the smoke through the brown leaves sere
 Blinded your dear eyes that you wept;

Was it not I that caught you then,
 And kiss'd you on the saddle-bow?
Did not the blue owl mark the men
 Whose spears stood like the corn a-row?

This Oliver is a right good knight,
 And must needs beat me, as I fear,
Unless I catch him in the fight,
 My father's crafty way—John, here!

Bring up the men from the south gate,
 To help me if I fall or win,
For even if I beat, their hate
 Will grow to more than this mere grin.

104

That with this bright believing band
   I have no claim to be,
That faiths by which my comrades stand
   Seem fantasies to me,
And mirage-mists their Shining Land,
   Is a strange destiny.

Why thus my soul should be consigned
   To infelicity,
Why always I must feel as blind
   To sights my brethren see,
Why joys they've found I cannot find,
   Abides a mystery.

Since heart of mine knows not that ease
   Which they know; since it be
That He who breathes All's Well to these
   Breathes no All's-Well to me,
My lack might move their sympathies
   And Christian charity!

I am like a gazer who should mark
   An inland company
Standing upfingered, with, 'Hark! hark!
   The glorious distant sea!'
And feel, 'Alas, 'tis but yon dark
   And wind-swept pine to me!'

Yet I would bear my shortcomings
  With meet tranquillity,
But for the charge that blessed things
  I'd liefer not have be.
O, doth a bird deprived of wings
  Go earth-bound wilfully!

.   .   .   .   .

Enough. As yet disquiet clings
  About us. Rest shall we.

105

'You never attained to Him?' 'If to attain
  Be to abide, then that may be.'
'Endless the way, followed with how much pain!'
    'The way was He.'

106

Thou art the Way.
Hadst Thou been nothing but the Goal,
   I cannot say
If Thou hadst ever met my soul.

   I cannot see—
I, child of process—if there lies
   An end for me,
Full of repose, full of replies.

   I'll not reproach
The road that winds, my feet that err.
   Access, Approach,
Art Thou, Time, Way, and Wayfarer.

107

'Christmas and whitened winter passed away,
  And over me the April sunshine came,
  Made very awful with black hail-clouds, yea

'And in the Summer I grew white with flame,
  And bowed my head down—Autumn, and the sick
  Sure knowledge things would never be the same,

'However often Spring might be most thick
  Of blossoms and buds, smote on me, and I grew
  Careless of most things; let the clock tick, tick,

'To my unhappy pulse, that beat right through
  My eager body. For a little word,
  Scarce ever meant at all, must I now prove

'Stone-cold for ever? Pray you, does the Lord
  Will that all folks should be quite happy and good?
  I love God now a little, if this cord

'Were broken, once for all what striving could
  Make me love anything in earth or heaven?
  So day by day it grew, as if one should

'Slip slowly down some path worn smooth and even,
  Down to a cool sea on a summer day;
  Yet still in slipping there was some small leaven

'Of stretched hands catching small stones by the way,
  Until one surely reached the sea at last,
  And felt strange new joy as the worn head lay

'Back, with the hair like sea-weed; yea all past
Sweat of the forehead, dryness of the lips,
Washed utterly out by the dear waves o'ercast,

'In the lone sea, far off from any ships!'

108

Striped with fierce wales of sunlight the brown idol
   gapes nonchalantly through disfeatured eyes,
while round his trunk bursts in green foam the tidal
   wave of hot creeping plant-obscenities.

He is as blank as those who worship, dumb
   as their dark minds, and does not care, nor know,
when the black chuckle, rubbed across the drum,
   drifts down as palpable as evil snow.

He is the image of their emptiness,
   the carvèd metaphor of minds untaught,
guessing, as we as pitifully guess
   at God, and bringing Him, like us, to naught.

And, while the victim flounders at his knees,
   the nameless god, to whom is sacrificed
the tortured blindness of the savage, sees
   beyond this tumult the slow tears of Christ.

109

I fear'd the fury of my wind
Would blight all blossoms fair and true;
And my sun it shin'd and shin'd,
And my wind it never blew.

But a blossom fair or true
Was not found on any tree;
For all blossoms grew and grew
Fruitless, false, tho' fair to see.

110

How should I your true love know
  From another one?
By his cockle hat and staff,
  And his sandal shoon.

He is dead and gone, lady,
  He is dead and gone;
At his head a grass-green turf,
  At his heels a stone.

White his shroud as the mountain snow,—
  Larded with sweet flowers;
Which bewept to the grave did go
  With true-love showers.

III

The wild winds weep,
And the night is a-cold;
Come hither, Sleep,
And my griefs unfold:
But lo! the morning peeps
Over the eastern steeps,
And the rustling beds of dawn
The earth do scorn.

Lo! to the vault
Of pavèd heaven,
With sorrow fraught
My notes are driven:
They strike the ear of night,
Make weep the eyes of day;
They make mad the roaring winds,
And with tempests play.

Like a fiend in a cloud,
With howling woe
After night I do crowd,
And with night will go;
I turn my back to the east
From whence comforts have increas'd;
For light doth seize my brain
With frantic pain.

112

'Christ keep the Hollow Land
   Through the sweet springtide,
When the apple-blossoms bless
   The lowly bent hill side.'

'Christ keep the Hollow Land
   All the summer-tide;
Still we cannot understand
   Where the waters glide:

'Only dimly seeing them
   Coldly slipping through
Many green-lipped cavern mouths
   Where the hills are blue.'

NOTES AND
INDEXES

Notes

NOTE ON THE TRANSCRIPTION

These poems were copied out from printed texts, rather than from memory. On May 8th, 1928, Lawrence wrote to Charlotte Shaw: 'My memory for things which I have read is almost nil. I read so fast, perhaps. You know that tiny anthology of poems I sent you? It travelled with me for years, and there is not a poem in it I have not read 50 times. Yet I do not know any verse of them well enough to write it down correctly.'

His transcription of the poems was generally accurate, except for certain idiosyncrasies. He omitted nearly all semicolons, replacing them by a colon or a comma. He also frequently omitted commas at the end of lines, and his internal punctuation was erratic. Another practice was to replace the form 'rever'd', 'prais'd', etc., by 'revered', 'praised'.

The poems were probably written out consecutively, as printed, except in the few cases where there are two poems on a page. Here the second was usually a later addition. No. 10 was included very much later than No. 9 (the handwriting and ink compare with No. 87 and later poems by William Morris). No. 13 was added long after No. 12 (probably in 1922 or 1923). No. 27, also by Morris, is a later addition, and so is No. 29, by Edward Thomas (possibly, judging by ink and handwriting, included with No. 81). No. 39 is a later addition, probably added with No. 53. No. 47 is written in a different ink from No. 46, and must have been added at least after No. 75. The same applies to No. 50. Before No. 75 Lawrence placed a red dot beside the beginning of each new stanza, but Nos. 10, 13, 50, 62, 65, 66, 67, 68 and 71–4 all lack these.

The anthology was begun in 1919, probably towards the end of the year. Excluding the later additions, Nos. 1 to 45 (approximately) were probably copied out during 1919–20. No. 68 was first published in 1922, and belongs to a second group of poems added just before his enlistment and during the early years of his service. No. 86 was included in April 1923, No. 98 in August 1924. It is uncertain when the eight poems following this were added, but Nos. 107–12 were added in India in 1927.

It is not easy to judge from the manuscript whether poems were written in on the same day, but changes in ink or handwriting may be significant. Lawrence used a medium-nib pen which, during the early 1920s, was usually filled with blue-black ink. He also often used a mapping pen and Indian ink (for example in the MS. of *Seven Pillars*). Some of the longer poems have been copied out with this type of pen. In later years he generally used Indian ink for all purposes. In the table which follows, I have summarized the evidence about ink and handwriting: 'b.m.p.' stands for 'black mapping pen'; otherwise a medium nib is assumed, and only the colour of ink is noted.

Poem No.		Poem No.	
1–4	blue-black	39 (later insertion) blue-black	
5	black	41	blue-black
6–14	blue-black	42	black
10 (later insertion) black		43–55	black fading to blue-black
13 (later insertion) black			
15	b.m.p.	47 (later insertion) black	
16	blue-black	50 (later insertion) black	
17	b.m.p.	56	black
18–19	blue-black	57–60	blue-black
20	b.m.p.	61	b.m.p.
21–5	blue-black	62–9	blue-black
27 (later insertion) black		70	b.m.p.
28–32	b.m.p.	71–8	blue-black
29 (later insertion) black		79–87	black
33–4	blue-black	88	blue-black
35	b.m.p.	89–90	b.m.p.
36–7	blue-black	91	blue-black
38–40	b.m.p.	92	black

Poem No.		Poem No.	
93	blue-black	103	black (handwriting
94–6	black		different from
97	b.m.p.		102)
98	black	104	blue-black
99–100	b.m.p.	105–6	b.m.p.
101	black	107	black
102	black (handwriting	108–10	b.m.p.
	different from 101) ·	111–12	black

1 JAMES ELROY FLECKER: Prologue to 'The Golden Journey to Samarkand'. Flecker became British Vice-Consul in Beyrout in the autumn of 1911. Lawrence met him there, and visited him on several occasions. In 1925 he drafted an essay on Flecker which was published posthumously (an edited text appears in *Men in Print*). Two passages bear directly on Flecker's writing:

' "What's this 'Georgian Poetry' book?" asked I once, disparaging in my innocence. "Oh," said he, "a collection of all our stuffs — jolly useful. Shows how much better a poet I am than my contemporaries." This was not panache on Flecker's part: he was wrapped up in poetics, making a wide, exact, skilful study of how other men had written. He left untouched no one of the sources of European verse. His education had given him scholarship to master ancient Greece and Rome. His profession had taught him some classical Arabic, some Turkish. His practice made him acquainted with modern Greek. French was a daily language to him …

'Some of the corrupt early stuff was I feel sure Herman Flecker's work:[1] I feel assured that "Flecker", the mature poet whom we know as F. was James Hellé[2] Flecker … as some of the early rococo stuff was rather Herman than James. It was the union of F. and his wife which wrought the miracle, which alloyed his too soft gold into a metal fit for our use.'

Flecker probably introduced Lawrence to contemporary poetry;

---

[1] Flecker's abandoned first name was Herman.
[2] Hellé Flecker was his wife.

for example, the work of Richard Middleton is praised in Flecker's letter of October 12th, 1912, to Edward Marsh;[1] Lawrence visited Beyrout that August, and wrote home shortly afterwards to obtain Middleton's work, singling out the same poem as that admired by Flecker.

The metaphor 'that calm Sunday that goes on and on' appears in several of Lawrence's post-war letters, particularly after the Peace Conference, and shortly before his retirement from the R.A.F. in 1935: 'For myself, I am going to taste the flavour of true leisure. For 46 years have I worked and been worked. Remaineth 23 years (of expectancy). May they be like Flecker's "a great Sunday that goes on and on." If I like this leisure when it comes, do me the favour of hoping that I may be able to afford its prolongation for ever and ever.' (B:L.H., p. 229.)

2 D. H. LAWRENCE: 'Ballad of a Wilful Woman'. 'D. H. Lawrence ... I can smell the genius in him: excess of genius makes his last book sickening: and perhaps some day the genius will burst through the darkness of his prose and take the world by the throat. He is very violent, is D.H.L.: violent and dark, with a darkness which only grows deeper as he writes on. The revelation of his greatness, if it comes, will be because the public grow able to see through his dark thinking ... because the public begin to be dark-thoughted themselves. D.H.L. can't make himself clear: he can't use the idiom of you and me. So often you find men like that, and sometimes the world grows up to them and salutes them as "kings-before-their-time ..." and sometimes nobody ever bothers about them at all, afterwards.' (22.viii.26 to C. F. Shaw.)

Lawrence wrote a review of *Women in Love, The Lost Girl* and *The Plumed Serpent*, published in the *Spectator* on August 6th, 1927, quoting the first two stanzas of Part II from 'The Ballad of a Wilful Women'. (At that time he was in India, so *Minorities* was probably his source.) 'Do you see the doubled "s" in each first and last line? There is the young Lawrence, his imagination playing lead to his mind. Appetite and self-education rushed him into growth. Ideas leaped in flocks, full-grown, into his work, too

[1] *Some Letters from Abroad* (Heinemann, London, 1930), p. 69.

quickly to be always clear, too grown to be always good company, one to the other. *The Rainbow* and *Women in Love* and *Aaron's Rod* stutter and stammer with the heat of the teacher who has felt something so exciting that he cannot delay to think it into its fitting words. Words upon words, he pours them out in a river ...' (The *Spectator*, 6.viii.27.)

A remark on *Lady Chatterley* is characteristic: 'I'm dreadfully sorry for a man who's gone right through life and found that it means no more than that at the end. Old Bridges, now, has just finished his longest poem, a philosophic poem, and is happy.' (3.vi.29 to Sir Edward Marsh.) Later, Lawrence wrote: 'Of course D.H. got all his values wrong. We all do, probably: but for me his values are hopeless, and his world utterly remote from mine. That's the great thing about an artist: by his means you can (dimly perhaps) apprehend other worlds and values. One's own worlds and values are the theme of all ordinary books ... The rarer a man's world, the more he is worthwhile, to us.' (4.iv.30 to C. F. Shaw.)

D. H. Lawrence's letters, however, he found greatly disappointing: 'I read them all, in daily doses extending over a fortnight. A sad reading, rather because D.H. wrote some lovely novels, and all of them came to me as they appeared, and I had a regard for the silly angry creature. And his letters lack generosity so sadly: couldn't he have said one decent thing about some other man of his profession?' (2.xii.32 to F. N. Doubleday, D.G., p. 755.)

'The Ballad of a Wilful Woman' is one of a series of autobiographical poems published under the title *Look! We have come through!* This is prefaced by the following 'Argument': 'After much struggling and loss in love and in the world of man, the protagonist throws in his lot with a woman who is already married. Together they go into another country, she perforce leaving her children behind. The conflict of love and hate goes on between the man and the woman, and between these two and the world around them, till it reaches some sort of conclusion, they transcend into some condition of blessedness.'

It is tempting to speculate that T. E. Lawrence's choice of this poem is related to the circumstances of his parents' life together, but such a theory seems improbable, for his parents' feelings were not his own experience and were wholly irrelevant to him at this time. In the Foreword to *Look! We have come through!* D. H. Lawrence wrote that the poems were 'intended as an essential story, or history, or confession, unfolding one from the other in organic development, the whole revealing the intrinsic experience of a man during the crisis of manhood ...' I believe that T. E. Lawrence saw in the poem a subtler and more personal relevance, and that the 'obvious' interpretation should be ignored.

4 ERNEST DOWSON: 'Vitae summa brevis spem nos vetat inco-hare longam'. '... when I think of lives for which I am very grate-ful: for poor Dowson, who wrote ten lovely poems, and died; for Rossetti, who wrote a few more, and died; for Coleridge, who wrote for two years, and then ran dry; why surely duration and bulk aren't the first considerations?' (17.v.28 to C. F. Shaw.)

'Beethoven was a very great man, and Wolf a small one. Milton, I think, was very great, and Dowson very small: but Dowson, *therefore* sang better. Singing is not a great art: it is incompatible with greatness, almost.' (9.xii.31 to C. F. Shaw.)

In late 1919 he sent a copy of this poem to Lionel Curtis noting that he thought 'Impenitentia Ultima' (No. 8) better.

6 LAURENCE HOUSMAN: 'Failure'. Lawrence did not like the fourth verse; in late 1919 he sent the first three to Lionel Curtis, noting against 'thus to have slipped unfamous from the crowd': 'in applying this line to T.E.L. "infamous" loc. curr.' He wrote out the entire poem on the verso of the Epilogue in the MS. of *Seven Pillars* (which he presented to the Bodleian Library in February 1923).

The first three verses also appear in a letter to Charlotte Shaw (18.viii.27) with the comment:

'I won't write the fourth verse. It should have ended the poem: it grizzles and mizzles, and is a feeble bleat.

> Two voices are there; one is of the deep
> And one is of an old half-dizzy sheep
> And "Housman" both are thine![1]

[1] Adapted from J. K. Stephen's parody of Wordsworth.

'If I were king of the world L.H. should be put in the Tower, and fed on thistles and beef-dripping, till he had cut out the weak line, above, and written a worthy last verse. The brute, to let a holy poem go limping on a short jury-leg.'

7 For Flecker, see note 1.

8 ERNEST DOWSON: 'Impenitentia Ultima'. (For Dowson, see note 4.) The first two lines of the second verse are quoted in *Seven Pillars*. (In the 'Oxford' draft the whole of this verse was included; Edward Garnett advised the cut.) The incident in *Seven Pillars* was a camel charge during which Lawrence inadvertently shot his mount in the back of the head:

'I was torn completely from the saddle, sailed grandly through the air for a great distance, and landed with a crash which seemed to drive all the power and feeling out of me. I lay there, passively waiting for the Turks to kill me, continuing to hum over the verses of a half-forgotten poem, whose rhythm something, perhaps the prolonged stride of the camel, has brought back to my memory as we leaped down the hill-side ... While another part of my mind thought what a squashed thing I should look when all that cataract of men and camels had poured over.

'After a long time I finished my poem, and no Turks came, and no camel trod on me ... I sat up and saw the battle over, and our men driving together and cutting down the last remnants of the enemy. My camel's body had lain behind me like a rock and divided the charge into two streams.' (S.P., Ch. LIII, p. 303.)

9 WILLIAM MORRIS: from *The Story of the Glittering Plain*. Lawrence's deep affection for the work of William Morris went back to his childhood. At Oxford and later he planned with Vyvyan Richards to set up a private press modelled on Kelmscott, and the ideals of craftsmanship, and the rejection of contemporary society implicit in the Pre-Raphaelite movement, appealed to him strongly. It is difficult to select from the great number of references to Morris, unquestionably Lawrence's favourite author, in his letters:

'Morris was a great poet: and I'd rather have written *The Well*

at the World's End or *The Roots of the Mountains* or *John Bull* or
The Hollow Land [from which the final poem in *Minorities* is
taken] than anything of the 19th Cent. except *War and Peace* or
Moby Dick. Sigurd and *The Dynasts* and *Paradise Lost* and *Samson*
and *Adam Cast Forth* [by C. M. Doughty] are the best long poems
in English. And Morris wrote 50 perfect short poems.[1] Why, the
man is among the very great! I suppose everybody loves one
writer, unreasonably. I'd rather Morris than the world.' (23.iii.27
to C. F. Shaw.) '... the charm and comfort of imperfection makes
up for most of the failures of the world. We admire the very great,
but love the less: perhaps that is why I would choose to live with
the works of William Morris, if I had to make a single choice.
My reason tells me that he isn't a very great writer: but then, he
wrote just the stuff I like ...' (October 1929 to C. F. Shaw.)

10   For Morris, see note 9.

12   JAMES ELROY FLECKER: 'The Pensive Prisoner'. (For Flecker
see note 1.) Compare this passage from *The Mint*, Part I, Chapter
4, p. 19: 'At ten-fifteen lights out; and upon their dying flash every
sound ceased. Silence and the fear came back to me. Through the
white windows streaked white diagonals from the conflicting arc-
lamps without. Within there ruled the stupor of first sleep, as of
embryos in the natal caul. My observing spirit slowly and deli-
berately hoisted itself from place to prowl across this striped upper
air, leisurely examining the forms stretched out so mummy-still
in the strait beds. Our first lesson in the Depot had been of our
apartness from life. This second vision was of our sameness, body
by body. How many souls gibbered that night in the roof-beams,
seeing it? Once more mine panicked, suddenly, and fled back to
its coffin-body. Any cover was better than bareness'.

13   JOHANN WOLFGANG VON GOETHE: from *Faust*, Act I
Scene 1. Volume I. of Lawrence's Dove's Press *Faust* is initialled
'J.H.R.'; i.e. 'J. H. Ross', his R.A.F. pseudonym between August
1922 and January 1923. In *The Mint*, Part II, Chapter 15, he men-
tioned reading *Faust* during the recruits' 'school' periods.

[1] See Nos. 10, 26, 27, 87, 92, 96, 103, 107 and 112.

In two letters to D. G. Hogarth, 13.vi.23 and 27.vi.23, Lawrence wrote about his decision to enlist. A postscript to the second reads: 'I feel I've explained myself so badly to you. Would Faust's phrase "von allem Wissensqualm entladen" be any good? It's a like case.' (D.G., p. 426.)

14 For Dowson, see note 4.

15 A. C. SWINBURNE: from a chorus in *Atalanta in Calydon*. On the voyage to Syria from England in 1913 'I came to know the early work of Swinburne better than before. He is quite good after all, though alas, like Browning long-winded to the extent of ultimate boredom. On the steamer however, where all passengers yawn their way along the decks between meals, he was very well.' (25.viii.13 to his mother, H.L., p. 261.) This opinion evidently endured, for in May 1927 he made a very similar remark about Swinburne and Browning to Robert Graves (see B:R.G., p. 44).

This is one of two poems in *Minorities* (the other is Sir William Watson's 'The Great Misgiving', No. 35) which contain the metaphor of the third verse in the dedication poem to *Seven Pillars*:

> Love, the way-weary, groped to your body, our brief wage
> >> ours for the moment
> Before earth's soft hand explored your shape, and the blind
> >> worms grew fat upon
> >>> Your substance.

16 HENRY CUST: 'Non Nobis'. Henry Cust was the uncle and friend of Ronald Storrs, Lawrence's colleague in Arabia. In Lawrence's copy of the *O.E.V.* this poem is dated 22.xi.17. Lawrence was at Azrak on this date (see Chapter LXXXI of *Seven Pillars*), two days earlier he had been captured during a reconnaissance at Deraa, and brutally treated by the Turks. On the morning of the 21st he escaped, and returned to Azrak, but could not face the prospect of a winter's diplomacy there with the smooth northern townspeople who now came to make contact with the Arab forces. Instead he set out on November 23rd for Akaba.

18　JOHN KEATS: 'La Belle Dame sans Merci'. 'I think [Rupert] Brooke's technique as good as Keats', but his sense of the taste of words was less fine: and his native irony restrained him from the sugary-pictures of Keats. It restrained him too much, so that it was seldom musical: whereas Keats when his self-criticism held back from the sugar, had almost no likely fault to avoid. Art creation is avoidance as much as it is presentation. And it's interesting to see Keats' growth in force (and decline in sweetness) from *Endymion* to *Hyperion*.' (1922 to V. Richards)

19　RUDYARD KIPLING: 'A Dedication'. Kipling was interested in Lawrence briefly after the First World War, but for political, not literary, reasons. 'As you say, a queer fish, Kipling. Very censorious, apparently: and he lives in such a glass-house. Twice he sought me out, and spoke very much good of me. Then he read the *Seven Pillars*: and dropped me like a stale egg.' (20.iii.28 to C. F. Shaw.) For Kipling's letters to Lawrence, see *Letters to T. E. Lawrence* (Cape, London, 1962).

In Lawrence's copy of *The Oxford Book of English Verse* this poem is dated 17.vii.17. On this date Lawrence was on board H.M.S. *Dufferin*, sailing from Cairo to Jiddah. Akaba had fallen, and in Cairo Lawrence had secured official support for his plans to extend the Arab thrust northwards, using Akaba as base. The essential step that would enable the Arabs to enter Damascus had now been taken.

26　For Morris, see note 9.

27　For Morris, see note 9.

35　SIR WILLIAM WATSON: 'The Great Misgiving'. (See also note 15.) In Lawrence's copy of the *O.E.V.* this poem is dated 4.xi.17. On this date Lawrence arrived at Azrak on his way to attack the railway. Soon after the arrival of the Arab force it was found that Abd el Kader, whose co-operation was essential, had deserted to the enemy, 'with information of our plans and strength. The Turks, if they took the most reasonable precautions, would trap us at the bridge. We took council ... and decided to push on none the less, trusting to the usual incompetence of our enemy. It was not a confident decision. While we took it, the sunshine seemed less lambent, and Azrak not so far aloof from fear.' (S.P., Ch. LXXV, p. 415.)

36 SAMUEL TAYLOR COLERIDGE: from 'Youth and Age'. Lawrence quite frequently quoted, or misquoted, a passage by Coleridge, from the side notes to the *Ancient Mariner*. 'And everywhere the blue sky belongs to them [the stars], and is their appointed rest and their native country and their own natural homes, which they enter unannounced, as lords that are certainly expected, and yet there is a silent joy at their arrival.' On one occasion, after a particularly corrupt allusion to this passage, Lawrence wrote: 'Poor Coleridge would complain that I'd spoiled his best prose sentence. He wrote so little that was quintessential: and a cargo of dross.' (30.x.28 to C. F. Shaw.)

38 JAMES THOMSON: 'Sunday up the River', XVIII. Section XVIII appeared in the *O.E.V.* titled 'The Vine'. The next extract in *Minorities* is a later addition, probably included at the same time as Nos. 53 and 55 (all from this poem). On 24.ix.22 Lawrence wrote to Robert Graves: 'By the way James Thomson's *Sunday up the River* is most excellent, isn't it?' (B:R.G., p. 21). Nos 39, 53 and 55 were included at approximately this date.

39 For Thomson, see note 38.

42 SIEGFRIED SASSOON: 'Everyone Sang'. On March 19th, 1929, Lawrence wrote to Sir Edward Marsh declining an invitation to present the Hawthornden prize to Sassoon: 'I hope S.S. will understand. I enjoy his work, because it touches nearer to my own train of mind than the work of anyone else publishing. Every verse of his makes me say "I wish to God I'd said that": and his fox-hunting gave me a shock of astonishment that he was so different and so good to know. If I was trying to export the ideal Englishman to an international exhibition, I think I'd choose S.S. for chief exhibit. Only I wouldn't dare, really, to give him a

prize. Some day, perhaps, if I wrote more, I might qualify for one at his hands.' (D.G., p. 644.)

'Sassoon comes out on top of all us war-timers, I think. More vigour, more grace and swiftness of movement, more fire and heat—that's in his poetry—and more tranquil charm, in his prose. S.S. strikes me as probably a great writer, all in all.' (18.x.30 to William Rothenstein, D.G., pp. 703–4.)

There is an allusion to this poem in *Seven Pillars*, Ch. XXIII, p. 140, where Lawrence describes the Arab army setting out for Wejh: 'Everyone burst out singing a full-throated song in honour of Emir Feisal and his family.'

43 For Keats, see note 18.

44 SIEGFRIED SASSOON: 'Limitations'. (For Sassoon, see note 42.) In December 1919 Sassoon wrote out three poems in Lawrence's copy of *Picture Show*. These were 'Limitations', 'Early Chronology' and 'Phantom', which appeared in the American edition of this collection.

46 For Sassoon, see note 42.

47 For Sassoon, see note 42.

48 D. G. ROSSETTI: 'Sunset Wings'. 'Rossetti was a most marvellous creature. You find some of the roots of Morris, in him.' (8.v.28 to C. F. Shaw.)

'Rossetti's poetry is so wonderful ... Only *not* the ballads. They are (with the beastly Jenny, a mawkish poem) his weakest stuff. Rossetti was a very great poet: and his poetry was much greater than himself.' (30.x.28 to C. F. Shaw.)

'They are writing apologetically of Rossetti, in the papers, everywhere. He was a magnificent poet. Morris is half-praised. Morris was a giant. Somebody said that Dowson wasn't a great poet; or Flecker. God Almighty! Must everyone be as seven-leagued as Milton and Byron and Hardy? The English world is full of wonderful writing, by live men and dead men.' (14.vi.28 to David Garnett, D.G., p. 612.)

51 ANON (Christ Church MS.): 'Preparations'. Mentioned in a letter of 27.vi.23 to Lionel Curtis. (D.G., p. 421.)

52 A. H. CLOUGH: 'Say not the Struggle Nought Availeth'. As recounted in the Introduction, when Lawrence gave *Minorities* to Charlotte Shaw in 1927, he told her that 'Its poems have each of them had a day with me. That little hackneyed Clough, for instance, about light coming up in the west also: I read that at Umtaiye, when the Deraa expedition was panicking and in misery: and it closely fitted my trust in Allenby, out of sight beyond the hills.' (17.xi.27 to C. F. Shaw.) This poem is dated 19.ix.18 in Lawrence's copy of the *O.E.V.* The Arab forces were now subjected to Turkish air attack, which demoralized them greatly. Lawrence flew to Palestine on September 20th and secured two Bristol fighters from Allenby to provide air cover.

53 For Thomson, see note 38.

54 For D. G. Rossetti, see note 48.

55 For Thomson, see note 38.

56 For Swinburne, see note 15.

58 For Thomson, see note 38.

59 For D. G. Rossetti, see note 48.

60 For Thomson, see note 38.

61 For Swinburne, see note 15.

63 For D. G. Rossetti, see note 48.

64 For Thomson, see note 38.

65 JOHN DAVIDSON: from 'The Last Journey', epilogue to *The Testament of John Davidson*. 'Dowson wrote some glorious poems. Davidson was bigger but not so good: worthier, because he tried his hardest, and burst in the effort.' (31.v.25 to C. F. Shaw.) On another occasion Lawrence had mentioned Davidson in a facetious aside about James Barrie: 'Also he is Scotch, and therefore cannot be expected to be an absolute artist. Will you quote John Davidson against me? His Testaments are on my side.' (29.xi.24 to C. F. Shaw; Lawrence was himself partly Scots on his mother's side.)

68 A. E. HOUSMAN: 'Eight O'Clock'. This poem was first published in October 1922; Lawrence enlisted in the R.A.F. in August 1922, and although he could not have known the poem then, it seems to have fitted his feelings closely. Early in November he told Robert Graves that the night before he joined up 'I felt like a criminal waiting for daylight' (B:R.G., p. 23). There is a distinct echo of the poem in Chapter 3 of *The Mint*, which describes his first afternoon at the training depot, having already committed himself to service, yet before the oath, and issue of uniform, and subjection to discipline.

'They licensed us to wander where we pleased (within gates) through the still autumn afternoon. The clouded breadth of the fallen park, into which this war-time camp had been intruded, made an appeal to me ...

'The particular wilderness of the Pinne's banks seemed ... forbidden to troups: in its sallows sang a choir of birds. From the tall spire (where it pricked black against the sky on the ridge behind the pent-roofed camp) fell, quarter by quarter, the Westminster chimes on tubular bells. The gentleness of the river's air added these notes, not as an echo, but as an extra gravity and sweetness, to its natural sounds and prolonged them into the distances, which were less distant than silvered with the deepening afternoon and the mists it conjured off the water. The dragging rattle of electric trains and trams, outside the pale, emphasised the aloof purposefulness in which so many men were cloistered here.' (Mint, I, Ch. 3, pp. 16–17.)

69 For D. G. Rossetti, see note 48.

70 ALGERNON SWINBURNE: 'Super Flumina Babylonis'. (For
Swinburne, see note 15.) In the Epilogue to *Seven Pillars* Lawrence
wrote: '*Super Flumina Babylonis*, read as a boy, had left me longing
to feel myself the node of a national movement.' In the manuscript
of *Seven Pillars* presented to the Bodleian Library in 1923 this
remark does not appear in the Epilogue, but immediately after it
Lawrence wrote out a stanza from the poem:

Not the light that was quenched for us, nor the deeds that were
Nor the Ancient days,
Nor the sorrows not sorrowful, nor the face most fair
Of perfect praise.

71 For Davidson, see note 65.

72 PERCY BYSSHE SHELLEY: 'The World's Great Age Begins
Anew'. This poem is dated 15.iv.18 in Lawrence's copy of the
O.E.V. This was the day of the failure before Maan, described in
Chapter XCIV of *Seven Pillars*.

75 For D. G. Rossetti, see note 48.

76 For Davidson, see note 65.

78 JOHN CROWE RANSOM: 'The Lover'. Taken from *Poems
about God* (New York, 1919), the poem appeared in a revised form
in *Grace after Meat* (London, 1924), which was also in the Clouds
Hill library.

79 For Flecker, see note 1.

80 W. B. YEATS: 'A Faery Song'. 'Yeats is a dismal poet. Very
good: Oh very good: with, like Wordsworth a congenital in-
ability to write a good poem. He lacks vulgarity, in him, and con-
sequently lacks the sense to avoid vulgarity, and sentiment, which
is the female of vulgarity ...' (21.iv.27 to C. F. Shaw.)

In 1932, however, Lawrence wrote: 'W.B. is a lovely poet. His later work gets rarer and finer. It has lost tune and won such depth and fineness. A man who can surpass his youth, as he grows older, is a man of size.' (April 15th to C. F. Shaw.)

82 THOMAS HARDY: 'To the Moon'. On March 20th, 1923, Lawrence wrote to Robert Graves to ask whether he could arrange an introduction to Thomas Hardy, who lived near Dorchester, within easy reach of the Tanks Corps Depot at Bovington: 'He's a proper poet and a fair novelist, in my judgment, and it would give me a feeling of another milestone passed if I might meet him ...' (B:R.G., p. 25.) Five days later he wrote to Mrs Hardy, at Graves' suggestion, commenting that 'The Dynasts and the other poems are so wholly good to my taste'. On April 7th Lawrence called at Max Gate, but it was not until September that he was able to sum up his feelings about Hardy in a letter which he wrote with great care to Robert Graves:

'The truth seems to be that Max Gate is very difficult to seize upon. I go there as often as I decently can, and hope to go on going there so long as it is within reach: ... but description isn't possible. Hardy is so pale, so quiet, so refined into an essence: and camp is such a hurly-burly. When I come back I feel as if I'd woken up from a sleep: not an exciting sleep, but a restful one. There is an unbelievable dignity and rightness about Hardy: he is waiting so tranquilly for death, without a desire or ambition left in his spirit, as far as I can feel it: and yet he entertains so many illusions, and hopes for the world, things which I, in my disillusioned middle-age, feel to be illusory. They used to call this man a pessimist. While really he is full of fancy expectations.

'Then he is so far-away. Napoleon is a real man to him, and the country of Dorsetshire echoes that name everywhere in Hardy's ears. He lives in his period, and thinks of it as the great war: whereas to me that nightmare through the fringe of which I passed has dwarfed all memories of other wars, so that they seem trivial, half-amusing incidents.

'Also he is so assured. I said something a little reflecting on Homer: and he took me up at once, saying that it was not to be despised: that it was very kin to *Marmion* ... saying this not with a grimace, as I would say it, a feeling smart and original and modern, but with the most tolerant kindness in the world. Conceive a man to whom Homer and Scott are companions: who feels easy in such presences.

'And the standards of the man! He feels interest in everyone, and veneration for no-one. I've not found in him any bowing-down, moral or material or spiritual.

'Any little man finds this detachment of Hardy's a vast compliment and comfort. He takes me as soberly as he would take John Milton ... , considers me as carefully, is as interested in me: for to him every person starts scratch in the life-race, and Hardy has no preferences: and I think no dislikes, except for the people who betray his confidence and publish him to the world.

'Perhaps that's partly the secret of that strange house hidden behind its thicket of trees. It's because there are no strangers there. Anyone who does pierce through is accepted by Hardy and Mrs Hardy as one whom they have known always and from whom nothing need be hid.

'For the ticket which gained me access to T.H. I'm grateful to you — probably will be grateful always. Max Gate is a place apart: and I feel it all the more poignantly for the contrast of life in this squalid camp. It is strange to pass from the noise and thoughtlessness of sergeants' company into a peace so secure that in it not even Mrs Hardy's tea-cups rattle on the tray: and from a barrack of hollow senseless bustle to the cheerful calm of T.H. thinking aloud about life to two or three of us ...' (8.ix.23 to R. Graves, B:R.G., pp. 26–7.)

83 WALTER DE LA MARE: 'Arabia'. A poem admired by Flecker and advocated by him to Edward Marsh for inclusion in the *Georgian* anthology (see note 1 for reference to this letter). Lawrence thought that 'The De la Mare phrase "Dark-haired, dim-silked musicians" is the ne plus ultra of minor poetry' (the phrase is misquoted in this letter of 21.iv.27 to Charlotte Shaw). He used it in his draft essay on Flecker written in 1925: 'It wasn't the fakir, the pilgrim, the hermit, the ascetic of the East, nor the poor man who called to Flecker's spirit. By instinct, by taste, by upbringing, by inheritance his was the town-life of rich Syria, the satins and

silks, perfumes, sweetmeats, grocers and Syrian boys. Dim-silked, dark-haired musicians ...'

It is sometimes said that Lawrence hated Arabia by the end of the desert campaigns. Had that been the case, the inclusion of de la Mare's poem in *Minorities* would seem strange. In May 1930 Lawrence wrote to Frederic Manning: 'I wake up now, often, in Arabia: the place has stayed with me much more than the men and the deeds. Whenever a landscape or colour in England gets into me deeply, more often than not it is because something of it recalls Arabia. It was a tremendous country and I cared for it far more than I admired my role as a man of action.' (D.G., pp. 692–3.)

85 For Yeats, see note 80.

86 ROBERT GRAVES: 'A Forced Music'. Lawrence met Graves at All Souls early in 1920. For an account of this meeting and of their later friendship, see *Friends* and *T. E. Lawrence to his Biographer Robert Graves*. Graves wrote: 'Lawrence was for years the only person to whom I could turn for practical criticism of my poems. He had a keen eye for surface faults, and though I did not always adopt his amendments, it was rarely that I did not agree that something was wrong at the point indicated.' (B:R.G., p. 10.)

It was through Graves that Lawrence came to know Siegfried Sassoon, Edmund Blunden, Robert Bridges, Thomas Hardy and a number of other poets.

In April 1923 Lawrence wrote to him: '*Whipperginny* fell like a star into the darkness of this camp and I have been reading it in gobbets ever since. There's a Minority in it—*A Forced Music*.' (B:R.G., p. 22.)

87 For Morris, see note 9.

88 For Hardy, see note 82.

91 WILLIAM BLAKE: 'Song'. Blake is first mentioned by Lawrence in a letter written on August 2nd, 1908. Lawrence's reaction to his work was expressed vividly in 1927, at much the time that the four Blake poems were included in *Minorities* (see also Nos.

94, 109 and 111): 'Blake was mad: I'm near enough to madness to maintain that stoutly against Yeats and A.E. and all the children of light. Blake was mad, in the eyes of the law, and of medicine, and literal judgment. But this madness did his sane work all the violent good in the world … Thank heavens Blake never alloyed his gold with dross. It's either rubbish or perfection. Coleridge, a little bit like, in this way of division. But Blake was fey.' (14.iv.27 to C. F. Shaw.)

In another letter, Lawrence commented: 'Blake said "Bosom" (singular) to avoid having so many "s" (*sic*) in the line: and "universes" because "a universe" would not fit his rhythm. Blake wasn't ever subtle in word, like that. He wrote flowingly.' (21.viii.28 to C. F. Shaw.)

92 For Morris, see note 9.

93 For Hardy, see note 82.

94 For Blake, see note 91.

96 For Morris, see note 9.

97 THOMAS HARDY: final chorus from *The Dynasts*. (For Hardy, see note 82; for *The Dynasts*, see note 9.) Lawrence persuaded Hardy to autograph his copy of *The Dynasts*, which is now in the library of All Souls College, Oxford. Hardy wrote: 'Colonel Lawrence: from Thomas Hardy'; Lawrence added 'To T. E. Shaw for his comfort in camp from Lawrence'. (F., p. 490.)

98 F. L. LUCAS: 'Skias Onar'. This poem was first published in the *New Statesman* on August 9th, 1924. On September 29th Lawrence wrote to E. M. Forster: 'Who is F. L. Lucas, by whom have been two excellent poems lately in the *New Statesman*: and who wrote two excellent prose sketches in the defunct *Athenaeum*, just before it defuncked? Really excellent, I mean: a sure, rounded, polished, fluent, fluting voice. Really, really good.' (D. G., p. 467.)

In 1929 the Hogarth Press published *Time and Memory*, a collection of Lucas's poems. Lawrence wrote to David Garnett:

'Lately I've been reading Lucas' poems. They are so low-toned, and they creep in and over my spirit like lianas. First of all I saw heaps of faults: now I can't change a word or line. Very subtle they are. I feel that they aren't dynamic enough. There is a lack of sharp edges. Yet when I read them they still criticism in me. It's like parts of Kipling, in that. One curses K. till one reads him. I don't curse Lucas: but in my memory he isn't as good as re-acquaintance convinces me he is. I think I've been through the book about 20 times, and can't place it in myself. I like them awfully. It's like hearing myself speak perfectly, on every other page. He says just what I've felt inarticulately.' (18.iv.29 to David Garnett.)

99 JAMES STEPHENS: 'The Snare'. Lawrence evidently read James Stephens's poetry in the early 1920s, commenting in 1925 that he was 'v. good. His last poems contained three excellent bits. Also an earlier lovelier thing about a snared rabbit.' (9.xii.25 to C. F. Shaw. *A Poetry Recital*, 1925, does not contain 'The Snare', which had been published long before.) The previous year he had written of his public reputation: 'I know the reverse of that medal, and hate its false face so utterly that I struggle like a trapped rabbit to be it no longer.' (26.iii.24 to C. F. Shaw.)

Then in January 1926 Lawrence read *The Crock of Gold* with mixed reactions, but 'I took up his last little book of poems, and found him writing cleanly, beautifully, modestly, not pretending to be a greater poet than he is. The poetry is quite beautiful.' He found Stephens's prose pretentious: 'the writing my own book and the reception it has had, have driven my perverse mind to hate pretence in prose. You can't pretend in poetry. It decays into Noyes. In prose you can swindle half the people half the time ... Cold water, exposure to wind and rain, low company, that's what I'd prescribe for him if I were his doctor. He has them, almost, in his poetry.' (4.i.26 to C. F. Shaw.)

Two years later Lawrence was again critical of *Etched in Moonlight* (a collection of short stories), and concluded: 'Stephens can't ever leave a big thing alone. He does small things like an artist, and then cracks up, just when he should show himself something more ... To see such stuff spoilt: stuff which only he can produce.

All his books have been the same: from *The Charwoman's Daughter* upward. Only the poems are clean.' (26.iv.28 to C. F. Shaw.)

In 1929 Lawrence met Stephens at Lady Astor's: 'He was most interesting and extraordinary: quite un-worldly, inhuman, and impossible, but so sensitive and so right. It was a curious experience. How, with those ambitions, he can miss his target as often as he does, in prose and verse, amazes me. I suppose he aims so high that often he can't see his mark, himself: and of course no one else suspects there's a mark there.' (5.iv.29 to C. F. Shaw.)

101 HILAIRE BELLOC: from 'Stanzas written on Battersea Bridge'. 'Belloc *is* very nearly a great man: he is also, as nearly, a bad man.

'It is so hard for a Catholic to be honest: and Belloc is anti-Semitic, in the continental sense, and polyglot. He worships secular Rome, as well as spiritual Rome. Oh, he is very dangerous. The most able pen-for-hire in England. His history is interesting, as special pleading all the way. His feud against Henry VII delights me. If so great an enemy can find so little fault, then indeed Henry VII was a great ruler, though a mean fellow ...

'Belloc's best things are written in verse, I fancy: *The Road to Rome*[1] is delicious. His praise of wine reads well: but have you ever seen his paunch? Wine and food have made him disgusting, and the need to earn enough to slake his greed has led him to do unworthy work. And this he would not have fallen to, unless he had had a cheap streak in him. Nobler, many times, is poor Ernest Dowson, or poor Francis Thomson, in the gutter. At least they were drunkards. Belloc is a tippler.' (8.v.28 to C. F. Shaw.)

103 For Morris, see note 9.

104 THOMAS HARDY: 'The Impercipient', subtitled 'At a Cathedral Service'. A. W. Lawrence described his brother as 'religious by temperament and without a creed' (F., p. 594). Lawrence's fundamental belief is reflected both in his letters and in *Minorities*; yet despite the rigorous church and Sunday school attendance of

[1] The correct title is *The Path to Rome*.

263

his upbringing, he became a strong critic of formal religion. On April 14th, 1928, he wrote bitterly to William Rothenstein: 'I regret Hardy's funeral service. Mrs Shaw sent me a copy. So little of it suited the old man's nature. He would have smiled, tolerantly, at it all: but I grow indignant for him, knowing that these sleek Deans and Canons were acting a lie behind his name. Hardy was too great to be suffered as an enemy of their faith: so he must be redeemed. Each birthday the Dorchester clergyman would insert a paragraph telling how his choir had carolled to the old man "his favourite hymn". He was mild, and let himself be badgered, out of local loyalty. "Which hymn would you like for to-morrow Mr. Hardy?" "Number 123" he'd snap back, wearied of all the non-sense: and that would be his favourite of the year, in next day's *Gazette*.' (D.G., p. 582.)

107 WILLIAM MORRIS: from 'The Defence of Guenevere'. (For William Morris, see note 9.) Lawrence re-read the early poems and prose stories of William Morris in the summer of 1927. Both Nos. 107 and 112 date from this period. On July 14th Lawrence wrote to Charlotte Shaw: 'Like you, the conclusion of every matter with me is the consolation that death is coming daily nearer. Some day we will be able, without any feeling of meanness, to lie back and rest

> Yea, all past,
> Sweat of the forehead, dryness of the lips
> Washed utterly out by the dear waves o'ercast
> In the lone sea, far off from any ships!'

108 HUMBERT WOLFE: 'The Harlot', I. This poem, taken from *Requiem*, was first published in April 1927. On June 10th, 1927, Lawrence wrote to Charlotte Shaw: 'Have you ever tried to read any of the poetry of Humbert Wolfe? It used not to be very interesting: but he has talent, and might develop passion. He put out another book lately. If you can borrow it, will you look at it for me, and see if it's worth reading?'
  Earlier that year (23.iii.27) he had told her that 'Humbert Wolfe has a fine pen, and good sense ... Sometimes admirable ...';

but later comments suggest that Lawrence thought *Requiem* the peak of Wolfe's achievement.

109   For Blake, see note 91.

110   WILLIAM SHAKESPEARE: from Hamlet, Act IV, Scene 5. 'There is more word-music in W.S. mouth than in all human mouths since. He couldn't say an absolutely ugly thing: though granted that the sound far surpasses the sense.' (5.xi.25 to C. F. Shaw.)

'I didn't call Shakespeare 2nd rate: only his intellect. He's the most consummate master of vowels and consonants: and the greatest poet. As a philosopher and moralist I have no abnormal respect for him: but the Elizabethan age was tempered rather than forged steel.' (1.xii.22 to Edward Garnett, D.G., p. 385.)

Ten years earlier Lawrence had written of the plays that 'the poetry, if anything, unfits them for presentation, since one cannot find a man worthy to do anything more than think of it.' (11.v.12 to his mother, H.L., pp. 205–6.)

111   For Blake, see note 91.

112   For Morris, see note 9.

Index of Authors

References are to poem numbers

Index of First Lines

References are to page numbers